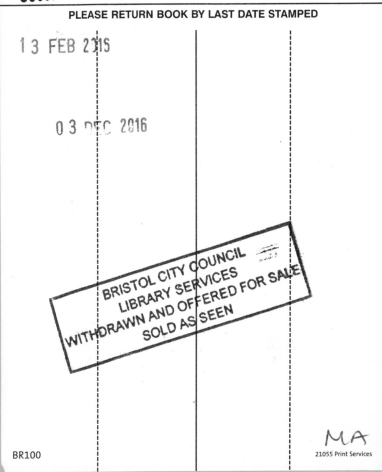

BREAD

BREAD

ERIC TREUILLE & URSULA FERRIGNO

Photography by

IAN O'LEARY

DK

LONDON, NEW YORK, MELBOURNE, MUNICH and DELHI

New edition

Editors Shannon Beatty, Penny Warren
Managing Editor Stephanie Farrow
Senior Art Editor Rosamund Saunders
DTP Designer Sonia Charbonnier

Original edition

Project Editor Julia Pemberton Hellums
Senior Editor Nicola Graimes
Editor David Summers
Project Art Editors Hilary Krag, Gurinder Purewall
Designer Rachana Shah
Senior Managing Editor Krystyna Mayer
Managing Editors Mary Ling, Susannah Marriott
Managing Art Editor Toni Kay
DTP Designer Karen Ruane
Production Manager Maryann Webster

First published in Great Britain in 1998 by
Dorling Kindersley Limited,
80 Strand, London WC2R 0RL
Penguin Group

A CIP catalogue record for this book is available
from the British Library.

Hardback ISBN 0 7513 0607 X

Paperback ISBN 0 7513 2584 8

Reproduced in Italy by GRB Editrice, Verona
Printed and bound in China by
L. Rex Printing Co. Ltd.

Discover more at
www.dk.com

CONTENTS

INTRODUCTION

In France and in Italy, where we come from, a meal is not a meal without bread. There, bread is taken very seriously. The daily visit to the bakery is a ritual that punctuates the rhythm of life. People choose their bread with special care and patronise the baker of their choice with an almost religious allegiance. It is said that the table is not laid until there is bread set on it. Bread is used to eat *with* as much as it is eaten: a piece of bread is used as a kind of secondary fork, and then is used to wipe the plate clean of every last morsel. Indeed culinary life, for many, begins with bread as mothers give their babies a hard crust to cut their teeth on.

All over the world, bread plays an important role in festivals and celebrations, traditions, and superstitions. Eric's father, like others of his generation, still marks the sign of the cross with the tip of his knife on the base of a loaf before he cuts it. Both of us clearly remember being warned as children not to place a loaf of bread top crust down on the table as it was sure to bring bad luck.

We were both privileged that our first experiences of making bread came early. Indeed, Eric's first contact with professional cooking was with bread; in his school holidays, he worked as a *mitron* – a baby baker – at *Le Fournil*, his uncle's *boulangerie* in South West France. Ursula remembers the hot summer evenings when her grandmother would light the wood-fired oven on the terrace of their family home in Campania. She recalls the sweet, yeasty fragrance of the seemingly magically growing dough and its soft, springy texture as she formed it into a thin round, for it was a family tradition that each person shape and top their own pizza.

When work drew us away from our homes to London, we were puzzled and shocked at the acceptance of mass-produced, inferior bread. It was our natural appreciation of bread with which we were raised that propelled us into baking bread at home for ourselves and then into teaching others how to do the same. Besides providing good food, something wonderful happens to your kitchen and your life when breadmaking becomes a regular activity. We hope that this book brings the same tremendous pleasure and satisfaction.

Eric   Ursula

THE FUNDAMENTALS OF BREADMAKING

MAKING BREAD REQUIRES little more than a pair of hands, an oven, and patience. The recipe for success is simple: time and warmth are all it takes to transform a few basic ingredients into a springy, silky dough that bakes to a crackly, crusted loaf. It is like most things, easy when you know how, with practice making perfect. If we had to choose one single phrase that we feel is essential to breadmaking, it would be this: *bread is alive*. It is a living, growing entity, and above all, the product of its ingredients and its surroundings; it responds, just as we do, to its environment – "treat rising dough as if it were human" advises an old English farmhouse cookery book. While we advocate the use of scales, timers and thermometers, remember that observation is the baker's traditional tool. The more you make bread, the better your bread will be. Your mistakes are rarely irreversible (*see pages 162–163* for problem solving) or inedible.

ESSENTIAL INGREDIENTS AND TECHNIQUES

Flour is the main ingredient of most breads, accounting for about three-quarters of the finished loaf. The flour you choose will give your bread its individual character. Mass-produced, highly refined brands will make an honest loaf, but we urge you to seek out organic flours from independent mills to experience the taste and texture of truly great homemade bread.

The choice of flour affects not only the quality of the baked bread but also the breadmaking process. Flour will absorb more, or less, liquid according to the variety of wheat that it was made from, where it was harvested, and how it was milled. Such variables are compounded by the humidity in the air – on a damp day, flour will absorb less liquid than on a dry one.

The quantities of liquid given in the recipes can never be more than guidelines or general indications. Our mixing technique (*see pages 44–45*) suggests that you hold back a proportion of liquid and add it as needed. This method acts as a safeguard against overly wet dough and the consequent need to add extra flour, which upsets the balance between flour, salt, and yeast.

If you require a little more liquid than stated in the recipe, do not hesitate to add it; your aim is to produce a dough conforming to the consistency specified in the recipe, be it firm, soft, or wet. Observing and understanding the condition of your dough, and what it requires, is the key to successful breadmaking.

THE IMPORTANCE OF TEMPERATURE

A warm kitchen is a perfect place for making bread. Ideally, ingredients should be at room temperature before mixing – except the yeast, which should be dissolved at body temperature, 37°C (98.4°F). Summer heatwaves or even storing flour in a cool larder must be brought into the equation, and you may find it necessary to use cooler or warmer water to correct the balance – bearing in mind that yeast is killed by temperatures over 54°C (130°F).

In the days before central heating, people used to take their dough to bed with them! Less eccentric rising spots during cold weather include a warm bathroom, an oven with the pilot light on, and a position near, but not too close, to a radiator, open fire, or stove. Choose a glass or plastic bowl when rising dough; metal conducts heat over-efficiently and you might find the dough rising unevenly and drying on the side closest to a nearby heat source. Use temperature to control the baking timetable. Decrease the water temperature and leave the dough in a cool spot in order to slow down the rising process to fit in with your schedule; the refrigerator is ideal for all-day or overnight rising. Remember to allow a couple of hours for the dough to return to room temperature (*see page 50*).

THE JOYS OF BREADMAKING

Breadmaking works miracles on all levels. The slow, rhythmic kneading is therapeutic, opening up the lungs and rib cage, and releasing stresses and strains with gentle efficacy. Watch as the warmth and pressure of your hands brings the yeast to life and transforms a few commonplace ingredients into a growing dough. Everybody loves the smell of bread as it is being made. The yeasty fragrance of the rising dough permeates the kitchen, only to be superseded by the delicious aroma of the bread baking. Enjoy the process of breadmaking as well as the results.

BAKING AT HIGH ALTITUDES

Altitudes above 1,067m (3,500ft) have a low atmospheric pressure; this causes bread dough to rise and prove more quickly than is indicated in the book's recipes. No adjustments are need to the ingredients, but keep an eye on the dough and do not allow it to increase in volume more than is specified.

Breads that rise too quickly will not develop. To prevent this, allow the dough to rise twice (*see page 50–51*) before shaping.

At altitudes over 914m (3,000ft), increase the baking temperature by 15°C (59°F). This extra heat is needed to help form the crust in the intial stages of baking and to prevent the bread from over-rising during its final minutes in the oven.

SUCCESSFUL BREADMAKING

The golden rule for measuring all baking ingredients is to always stick to one system, never to mix and match. Both metric and imperial measurements are given in this book. It is imperative that you choose one system and use it throughout the recipe.

All spoon measurements are level: 1 teaspoon equals 5ml (⅙fl oz); 1 tablespoon equals 15ml (½fl oz). All eggs used in the book are large unless otherwise specified. Unsalted butter should always be used for breadmaking unless otherwise specified.

Make sure that all the ingredients used are at room temperature; be sure to take eggs, butter, and milk out of the refrigerator in good time.

A GALLERY OF BREADS

A WORLD OF POSSIBILITIES IS REVEALED IN THIS

GALLERY OF BREADS, WHICH CELEBRATES A

TRULY UNIVERSAL FOOD. A MEAL IS NOT A MEAL WITHOUT

BREAD IN COUNTRIES AS DIVERSE AS ITALY, INDIA, MEXICO

AND FRANCE. A VARIETY OF TEXTURES AND TASTES ABOUNDS

TO DEFINE THIS GLOBAL CULINARY STAPLE. ILLUSTRATED

HERE IS A SELECTION OF BREADS FROM SOME OF THE

WORLD'S MOST FAMOUS BREADMAKING TRADITIONS.

FRENCH BREAD

AN 18TH-CENTURY FRENCH
BAKER KNEADS DOUGH IN
A WOODEN TROUGH

BREAD IS AT THE HEART of the French culinary experience, and once even defined social status – the long, elegant white *Baguette* was affordable only to stylish city dwellers and rustic breads, like *Pain de Campagne*, were staples of life in the country. Today, however, these country-style sourdough breads have captured the imagination of contemporary bakers from New York to Tokyo.

COURONNE

Bread shapes in France were often designed by the baker to satisfy the needs of his customers. The hole in the middle of this loaf makes it easy to carry over the arm like a shopping basket. As well as being practical, the loaf's shape increases the proportion of crust to crumb. *Recipe page 85.*

PAIN DE SEIGLE

In France, rye bread originated in mountainous regions like the Pyrenees and the Vosges, where it was a staple bread. Today, it is more often served in Parisian brasseries, thinly sliced and thickly buttered as an accompaniment to oysters. *Recipe page 93.*

PISTOLETS

These distinctively shaped rolls are traditional to Belgium and North Eastern France, where they are a Sunday breakfast treat. The characteristic indentation along the top of each roll is easily made with the handle of a wooden spoon. *Recipe page 79.*

PAIN DE CAMPAGNE

Made throughout France in innumerable shapes and sizes, *Pain de Campagne* varies by region as well as by baker. All these breads have thick, dark crusts liberally dusted with flour, giving them their characteristic two-tone appearance. *Recipe page 85.*

FOUGASSE

One of the 13 desserts traditional to a Provençal Christmas, *Fougasse* can now be bought all year round. This decorative, branch-shaped bread is flavoured and enriched with olive oil. Additional flavourings are often added to the bread dough – crisp bacon, chopped anchovies, or caramelized onions are very popular. *Recipe page 149.*

BAGUETTE

A crackly, golden crust and light, chewy interior are the signatures of this world-renowned, classic bread. The French say it is best to buy two loaves at a time, because one is always half eaten by the time it arrives home. *Recipe page 79.*

TORDU

From the Limousin, a rural region in the centre of France, *le tordu*, the "twist", is a popular shape. It is favoured by bread connoisseurs who prize crust as highly as crumb. *Recipe page 85.*

ITALIAN BREAD

A 16TH-CENTURY
VENETIAN BAKERY

AN ITALIAN TABLE is not dressed without bread. Renaissance paintings depict tables adorned with baskets of freshly baked bread and this appealing image is just as current today. Each region of Italy has its own distinctive style of cooking and breadmaking. The food of northern Italy is very rich and its ingredients reflect the historical wealth of this area. Delicate, light breads are made here. Southern Italian food is the food of a humbler people, and a luscious bread filled with cheese and vegetables serves as a meal in itself.

STROMBOLI

This southern Italian bread is stuffed with mozzarella, fresh herbs, and shallots. During baking, the generous filling erupts out of the indentations made in the bread's crust. Hence it is named after the volcanic island off the coast of Sicily. *Recipe page 106.*

SCHIACCIATA CON L'UVA

This Tuscan bread is made to celebrate the grape harvest. It is filled with wine-soaked raisins from the previous year's harvest and traditionally topped with the new season's grapes. *Recipe page 109.*

PANE DI RAMERINO

Enriched with olive oil and eggs, studded with raisins, and scented with fresh rosemary, this delicious bread is most commonly seen at the Tuscan breakfast table. *Recipe page 115.*

GRISSINI

From the city of Turin, these crispy breadsticks can be made as thin as a pencil or as fat as a cigar. Toppings vary from simple coarse salt to the seed or dried herb of your choice. *Recipe page 80.*

CIABATTA

Distinctive to the Emilia Romagna region of Italy, *Ciabatta* is now baked around the world. It was created as a light, airy textured bread to accompany the region's rich pasta and meat dishes. *Recipe page 90.*

BRITISH BREAD

**BAKING DAY IN A
19TH-CENTURY ENGLISH VILLAGE**

WHATEVER THE SHAPE, the typical British loaf has a soft, tender crumb and a crispy rather than crusty exterior, often liberally dusted with flour. Through the centuries, the unerring preference of the British people has been for loaves made from white wheat flour. Historically, fine white bread graced only the tables of the lords of the manor. There were separate guilds for bakers of white and brown breads and the saying "to know the colour of your bread" meant to know your place in society.

VICTORIAN MILK BREAD

Milk is an important ingredient in many British breads. The use of milk in place of water softens both the crumb and crust. This bread has a velvety texture and a golden, smooth exterior. Its fancy scroll shape is typical of the popular Victorian novelty breads. *Recipe page 76.*

BLOOMER

Half milk and half water are used to make this long, plump loaf with its crispy crust and light, tender crumb. A typically British shape, this deeply scored loaf dramatically expands or "blooms" during baking. *Recipe page 76.*

COTTAGE LOAF

The most distinctive British shape, the cottage loaf, is made by stacking a small, round loaf on top of a larger round and joining them by making a deep impression, traditionally formed with the baker's elbow. *Recipe page 73.*

GRANARY TIN LOAF

Granary bread is made with a blend of wheat and rye flours mixed with malted grains. It is the most recent addition to the family of British breads; its slightly sweet, nutty taste and moist texture make this loaf a favourite of both children and adults. *Recipe page 73.*

SCOTS BAPS

Baps are soft, flat rolls made all over Great Britain, but are mostly associated with Scotland. There they are traditionally eaten at breakfast and called morning rolls. *Recipe page 77.*

IRISH SODA BREAD

This everyday Irish bread is traditionally "baked" in a cast-iron pot set over the embers of an open fire. With a cake-like texture, this bread is made without yeast and is best eaten on the day it is baked. *Recipe page 141.*

EUROPEAN BREAD

**A 19TH-CENTURY
GERMAN BAKERY**

THE BREADS OF EUROPE fall into two categories – the hearty country breads eaten daily and the lighter, richer, more refined breads reserved for feasts and celebrations. The traditional country breads were rarely made with wheat flour alone, but also incorporated a common staple of the region: rye in Germany, corn in Portugal, and potatoes in Hungary. Wheat flour was an expensive and precious commodity and these healthful additions provided nourishing bulk to the everyday European loaf.

PULLA

This saffron-coloured, cardamom-scented bread wreath is the traditional Christmas loaf of Finland. No longer restricted to festive occasions, it is now baked and eaten all the year round. *Recipe page 150.*

LANDBROT

The name of this crusty rye bread translates literally as "bread of the land", and it is one of the few breads that is baked throughout Germany; a rarity in this intensely regional country that boasts 400 different kinds of bread. *Recipe page 92.*

BROA

Originally from the Minho Province in the north of Portugal, this corn bread is now eaten all over the country. Maize grows profusely in Portugal and is used in many of the native dishes. *Recipe page 78.*

HUNGARIAN POTATO BREAD

In Hungary, potatoes are a staple commodity. This traditional bread uses potatoes to add moisture and substance to the loaf, which is subtly spiced with aromatic caraway seeds. *Recipe page 103.*

PARTYBROT

Guests can help themselves to this inviting German bread. It serves as the perfect centrepiece to a party's buffet table. *Recipe page 120.*

AMERICAN BREAD

**AN 18TH-CENTURY
COLONIAL BAKER**

PIONEERS AND HOMESTEADERS who settled the Americas brought the breadmaking traditions of their native countries with them and adapted these to suit the rustic conditions of their new home. Without the system of communal bakeries that had existed in Europe since the Middle Ages, they established an important tradition of home-baking that still exists today. North America is famous for its unique sourdoughs and quick breads, which are made without the traditional yeast leaveners.

SAN FRANCISCO SOURDOUGH

The origins of this bread date back to California's gold rush. Prospectors carried with them a mixture of flour and water kept in a packet strapped to their waists, which fermented to produce a leaven for this chewy, tangy bread. *Recipe page 86.*

FAN TANS

Native to New England, these fancy shaped rolls also go by the name Yankee Buttermilk. They have a light and airy texture that complements a hearty stew or roast. *Recipe page 121.*

PARKER HOUSE ROLLS

Soft rolls are a Sunday dinner staple all over America. This unique shape was created and popularized by the Parker House Hotel in Boston during the late 19th century. *Recipe page 118.*

CINNAMON RAISIN BREAD

Enriched with milk and flavoured with an inner whirl of raisins, this bread is an all-American breakfast favourite. Served toasted and topped with butter and cinnamon sugar, it is a fond childhood memory. *Recipe page 123.*

CORN STICKS

A heavy skillet was used by early settlers to cook corn bread on the hearth. Here, the quick bread batter is baked in a cast-iron mould that forms it into small ears of corn. *Recipe page 142.*

EASTERN BREAD

THE IMPORTANCE OF BREAD in the Middle East cannot be overstated. In the Arab world, bread is revered as a gift from God and the staff of life itself. Honour is asserted with the vow "on my family's bread I swear to tell the truth"; contentment expressed by saying "his water jug is filled and his bread is kneaded". Bread is present at every meal, from the simplest snack to the grandest banquet, and indeed takes the place of cutlery throughout the region. The most common bread is flat with a hollow pocket in the middle, used for filling with salads, grilled meats, or any of the region's mouthwatering mezze.

LAVASH

It is said that *Lavash* originated in Armenia but it is also eaten throughout Lebanon, Turkey, and Syria. Rolled paper-thin, it is traditionally cooked in a large outdoor oven called a *tannur*. *Recipe page 134.*

PIDE

Recognized by its distinctive ridged pattern, golden crust, and topping of nigella seeds, *Pide* is traditionally prepared for the Muslim festival of Ramadan, when it is eaten to break the fast at sunset. It can be topped with fennel seeds instead of nigella seeds. *Recipe page 137.*

BARBARI

This light, crusty Persian bread is commonly served for breakfast in Iran, where it is topped with cheese and fresh herbs. When made with water instead of milk and sprinkled with sugar instead of seeds, the bread becomes a much-loved children's snack called *shirmal. Recipe page 136.*

PAIN TUNISIEN

With a tender crumb and crisp crust, this bread is made with semolina flour. Semolina is produced from durum wheat – a staple of North Africa that is widely used in breadmaking and to make the cracked grain, couscous. *Recipe page 135.*

PITTA BREAD

Pitta is the Greek name for a soft, oval- or round-shaped bread with a pocket-like hollow in the middle. It is made all over the region, where it also goes by its Arab name of *khubz. Recipe page 134.*

FESTIVE BREAD

PREPARING BREAD FOR A
17TH-CENTURY FESTIVITY

THE CUSTOM OF BAKING SPECIAL BREADS in honour of festive celebrations and religious holidays is an ancient one. In contrast to the plain, hearty loaves that comprise the traditional "daily bread", festive breads are usually made with the most expensive and highly prized ingredients – golden butter and eggs, aromatic spices and flavourings, and sweet, dried and candied fruits. These ceremonial breads are formed into traditional shapes that have special symbolic meanings. Some are now commonly served throughout the year and not just for an occasion.

PANETTONE

This rich, golden loaf from Milan is studded with sultanas and delicately perfumed with citrus peel. Its dome-shaped top is said to resemble the cupolas of the churches of its native Lombardy. *Panettone* is traditionally enjoyed at Christmas. *Recipe page 155.*

PAN DE MUERTO

Flavoured with orange and anise seeds, this sweet bread is baked on the Mexican Day of the Dead, when families honour their dead by visiting the graves with offerings of flowers and food. *Recipe page 152.*

BOLO-REI

Rich breads and cakes are traditional in southern Europe to celebrate the feast of the Epiphany on 6 January. This lavishly decorated "Kings' Cake", from Portugal, is shaped to symbolize the crowns of the Three Kings who are said to have visited the baby Jesus on this day. *Recipe page 154.*

CHALLAH

The golden, braided loaf traditional for the Jewish Sabbath is the most familiar shape. It is shown here coiled into a circle that symbolizes continuity, and is baked to celebrate the Jewish New Year, Rosh Hashanah. *Recipe page 150.*

BAKING ESSENTIALS

FLOUR, WATER, AND YEAST – THESE ARE THE ESSENTIAL INGREDIENTS OF BREADMAKING. WHEN BROUGHT TOGETHER WITH THE HELP OF YOUR HANDS, A FEW BASIC TOOLS, AND A HOT OVEN, THEY CAN BE TRANSFORMED INTO A WARM, FRAGRANT LOAF. THE BAKING ESSENTIALS ILLUSTRATED IN THIS SECTION REVEAL WHAT BREAD IS: A FEW SIMPLE INGREDIENTS ELEVATED BEYOND THEIR HUMBLE ORIGINS TO BECOME AN EVERYDAY MIRACLE.

NON-WHEAT FLOURS

FOR CENTURIES VARIOUS DRIED GRAINS and roots have been ground and used to make bread. Most flours and meals come from cereal plants ground from seeds, including those made from rye, oats, barley, and corn. The seeds vary in shape and size, but all have a similar structure to the wheat kernel and are ground in the same manner. These flours produce breads with different flavours, textures, and nutritional values. Wheat flour, with its high gluten content, is preferable for risen breads. Low-gluten and non-gluten flours must be mixed with at least 50 per cent wheat flour to make a properly risen bread, but the addition of a few tablespoons of one of these flours will deepen a bread's flavour.

PRINCIPAL CEREAL GRAINS

RYE PLANT

GRAIN   FLOUR

RYE
Ground from cleaned grains, this flour inhibits gluten development. Even a small addition, mixed with wheat flour adds a distinctive tang to any bread. Dark rye flour contributes a strong flavour, while light rye flour is milder and paler.

OAT PLANT

GROUTS   PINHEAD OATS   FLOUR

OATS
Oats that have been cleaned and hulled are called oat grouts. Pinhead oats are grouts that have been cut into two or three pieces. Oat flour is ground from groats and is gluten-free. It adds rich flavour and texture to a bread.

BARLEY PLANT

PEARL BARLEY   FLOUR

BARLEY
Barley seeds with the bran removed are called pearl barley, which is eaten in soups and stews. Barley flour is ground from pearl barley and is gluten-free. Mixed with wheat flour it adds a sweet, earthy flavour.

CORN PLANT

KERNELS   COARSE MEAL   FINE MEAL

CORN
Dried corn kernels are ground into three textures of meal – coarse, medium (called polenta), and fine. All are gluten-free and have a distinctive corn flavour.

OTHER HELPFUL TOOLS

PASTRY SCRAPER
A pliable, plastic scraper is ideal for handling sticky dough.

PASTRY BRUSH
An all-purpose boar-bristle brush is best for applying glazes and washes.

SCALPEL
Use to slash the top of a risen dough before baking (see page 62).

SCISSORS
Kitchen scissors can be used to create decorative slashes in dough (see page 62).

THERMOMETER CASE

INSTANT-READ THERMOMETER
Practical for checking water temperature when preparing yeast (see page 41).

SIEVE
A stainless steel sieve is best for sifting flours together.

ROLLING PINS
Wooden cylindrical rolling pins are best for shaping dough.

BREAD KNIFE
A serrated knife will penerate a hard crust and slice through bread cleanly.

APPLIANCES

ELECTRICAL EQUIPMENT can be useful for mixing and kneading bread doughs. While a food processor ensures thorough mixing and partial kneading of a dough, a heavy-duty mixer allows the baker to develop the full elasticity of a dough through constant kneading for a longer period of time. However, electric mixers and processors can overwork and overheat the dough when set on a high speed. See pages 66–67 for tips on how best to use them.

FOOD PROCESSOR

HEAVY-DUTY MIXER

BAKING

AFTER THE INGREDIENTS HAVE BEEN CAREFULLY MEASURED and mixed to the proper consistency, the final stages of breadmaking also require the same careful attention. Preheat the oven in advance and use an oven thermometer to check its accuracy. A kitchen timer ensures that you keep track of the baking time, as well as the rising and proving times. Heavy-gauge baking tins and trays are best, since they resist buckling in the oven at high heats and prevent loaves from burning at the bottom.

KITCHEN TIMER
A clearly marked kitchen timer with a loud alarm will ensure accurate baking, rising, and proving times.

OVEN THERMOMETER
A thermometer will detect any variations in oven temperature (see page 64).

CORN STICK PAN
Each of this cast iron tray's depressions shapes a single serving of corn bread.

LOAF TIN
A 1kg (2lb) tin made from medium-weight metal is most frequently used in this book.

TERRACOTTA TILES
These help to radiate heat evenly and retain moisture in the oven, producing superior, thick-crusted, free-form breads (see page 63).

WATER SPRAY
A fine-spray nozzle is advisable for adding moisture to the oven while a bread is baking. Avoid spraying the oven light or heating elements directly (see page 63).

MUFFIN TIN
Use a non-stick, American-style muffin tin with deep cups in muffin recipes.

BREAD BOARD
Wooden boards are best for slicing bread since they are kind to the serrated blade of a bread knife.

BAKING SHEET
Use a heavy-duty, non-flexible, metal baking sheet for free-form loaves and rolls.

BRIOCHE MOULDS
The sloping sides of these classic moulds induce a maximum final rise and height during baking.

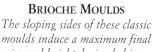

WIRE RACK
Use a wire rack to cool breads in order to prevent a soggy bottom crust (see page 65).

FRENCH BAGUETTE TRAY
This perforated tray ensures an even heat throughout baking, resulting in a crisp, golden outer crust.

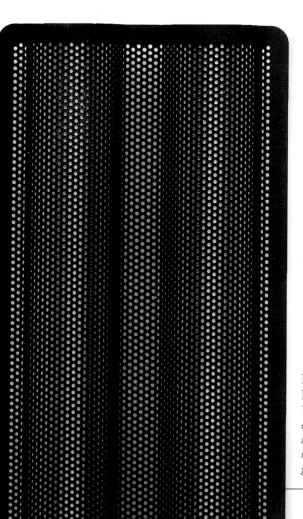

BASIC TECHNIQUES

T HE BASIC TECHNIQUES OF MAKING BREAD ARE

NOT COMPLICATED OR DIFFICULT TO FOLLOW.

SUCCESSFUL BREADMAKING, HOWEVER, REQUIRES TIME

AND PATIENCE – TRY NOT TO RUSH EACH STAGE. USE

THIS SECTION TO LEARN, FEEL, AND OBSERVE THE

PROCESSES THAT TRANSFORM BASIC INGREDIENTS

INTO A FINISHED LOAF. THIS IS YOUR HANDYWORK;

THE JOYS OF MAKING YOUR OWN BREAD BEGIN HERE.

HOW TO BEGIN

PRECISE PROPORTIONS and accurate quantities of leavener, water, and flour form the foundation upon which all good bread is based. The leavener, or rising agent, is the key to transforming simple ingredients into a risen bread. In this book, yeast, in either fresh or dried form, is the most commonly used leavener.

Yeast is a living organism, which relies on the sugar and starch present in flour to live and grow. Yeast produces carbon dioxide gas as it grows; this gas causes the bread dough to rise. Once activated in water, yeast will live for up to 15 minutes before it must be added to flour, the food source it requires to stay alive.

MEASURING THE INGREDIENTS

ACCURACY IS CRUCIAL when making bread. Use a kitchen scale clearly marked in metric or imperial measurements for weighing flour and other ingredients. Follow either metric or imperial measurements throughout the recipe. These two types of measurement are not interchangeable.

Choose one and stick with it throughout the recipe. Weigh all the ingredients carefully before you begin. Use a jug with clearly marked units for measuring liquids. Place on a flat surface and bend down to eye level with the measured mark to pour into the jug.

PREPARING THE YEAST

BOTH DRIED AND FRESH YEAST must be dissolved in tepid water to activate. This should be done just before adding the yeast to the flour. Avoid using metal bowls or utensils to prepare the yeast. Metal will sometimes impart an aftertaste to a yeasted mixture.

USING EASY-BLEND YEAST

TO USE EASY-BLEND YEAST, sprinkle it directly on to the flour. The yeast will activate once the liquid has been added. The standard method of mixing the dough must be followed since easy-blend yeast cannot be used with the sponge method (*see page 44–45*).

USING DRIED YEAST

1 Sprinkle dried yeast granules into a small, glass bowl containing tepid water; leave to dissolve for 5 minutes.

2 Once the yeast has dissolved stir the mixture with a wooden spoon. The yeast mixture is now ready to be added to the flour.

Granules will float on the surface and then sink

Foam indicates that the yeast has been activated

3 Gradually pour in half of the remaining liquid while mixing in the remaining flour from the sides of the bowl. As the water is added, the texture of the combined ingredients will change from a crumbly mixture to a shaggy, slightly sticky mass that will begin to come away from the sides of the bowl and form into a ball (*see below*). Add the rest of the water, as needed, to achieve the consistency specified in the recipe. The dough should remain soft and should not be too dry before it is transferred to a floured surface for kneading (*see pages 46–47*).

KNEADING

ESSENTIAL FOR AN OPEN-TEXTURED, full-flavoured bread, kneading performs a crucial function in preparing a dough to rise. First, it completes the mixing process by distributing the activated yeast throughout the dough. Continued kneading then allows the flour's proteins to develop into gluten, which gives dough the ability to stretch and expand.

Starches are broken down to feed the yeast, which creates bubbles of carbon dioxide gas. These bubbles cause the dough to rise. The actions shown are a guide to kneading a basic dough. Specific instructions, such as kneading a soft, wet dough (*see page 88*) or kneading coarse ingredients into a dough (*see page 99*), are demonstrated in the recipe section.

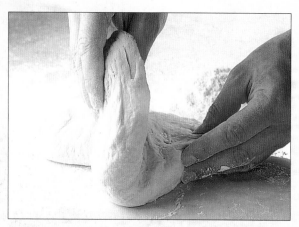

1 To begin kneading, shape the dough by folding one half over the other, bringing the top half towards you. Keep a little additional flour at the side to lightly dust the dough as you knead should it become difficult to handle. Use this extra flour sparingly.

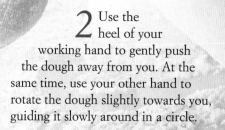

2 Use the heel of your working hand to gently push the dough away from you. At the same time, use your other hand to rotate the dough slightly towards you, guiding it slowly around in a circle.

3 Repeat these kneading actions, gently folding, pushing, and rotating the dough continuously for approximately 10 minutes, or until the dough achieves a firm touch, silky smooth surface, and elastic texture. Take time to work the dough slowly and firmly, but do not use excessive force. The dough will gradually become more elastic and easier to knead. Shape the dough into a ball for rising (*see pages 50–51*).

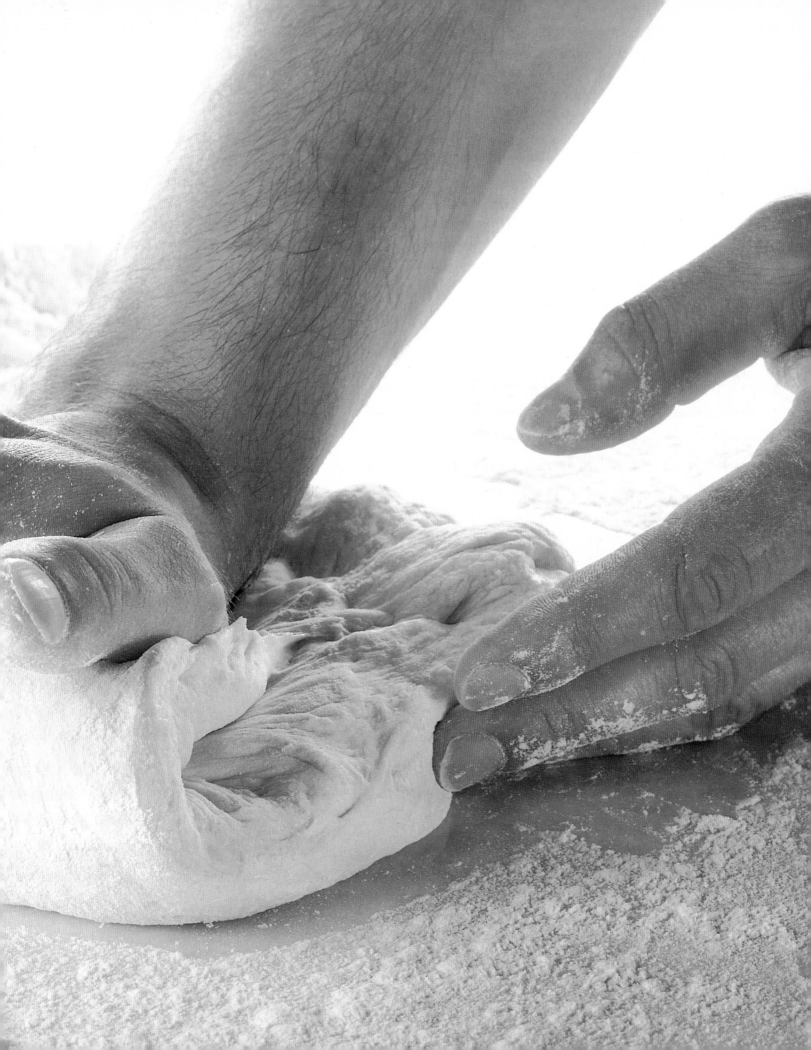

USING APPLIANCES

A FOOD PROCESSOR or heavy-duty electric mixer can be used as an alternative to mixing and kneading bread dough by hand. When using a food processor, check the capacity of your machine and, if necessary, divide the ingredients evenly so that you can mix and knead the dough in batches. Some kneading by hand will also be necessary. Bread dough can be made entirely in a heavy-duty electric mixer by using the mixing paddle to mix and the dough hook to knead. Be careful not to overwork the dough – high speeds stress the dough, causing it to rise incorrectly. Make use of the pulse button or low-speed setting on each appliance.

USING A FOOD PROCESSOR

1 Before starting, always fit the machine with a plastic dough blade. A metal blade will stress and overheat the dough.

2 Put the flour and any other dry ingredients into the work bowl; pulse to mix. With the machine running, pour in the yeasted water, followed by half of the remaining liquid. If using a starter, as specified in the recipe, add it to the work bowl at this point.

3 Add the rest of the water and continue to run the machine until the dough starts to form into a ball. Then leave the dough to rest in the machine for 5 minutes. Process the dough to knead for a further 45 seconds. Turn the dough out on to a lightly floured work surface and continue to knead by hand until smooth and elastic, about 3–5 minutes. Leave the dough to rise (*see pages 50–51*).

The dough should be firm and sticky before kneading by hand

HANDY TIPS

• *Use slightly cool water to dissolve the yeast to counterbalance the heat generated by the machine.*

• *After processing the dough in batches, turn them out on to a lightly floured work surface. Knead them together to form one piece of dough. Continue to knead until the dough is smooth and elastic.*

• *Use the pulse button often to prevent the machine from over-heating the dough. Do not run the machine continuously for more than 30 seconds at a time.*

USING A HEAVY-DUTY MIXER

1 Dissolve the yeast or make a starter as specified in the recipe and place directly in the mixing bowl. Use the paddle attachment to mix in half of the flour on low speed, then add the remaining liquid ingredients to the bowl.

2 Once the mixture forms into a loose batter, remove the paddle. Replace it with the dough hook. With the machine running, gradually add the remaining dry ingredients to the mixer.

3 Continue adding the dry ingredients until the dough pulls away from the sides of the bowl. Increase the speed to medium and work the dough until smooth and elastic, about 8–10 minutes. If the dough climbs up the hook, stop the machine, push it back down, and continue. Remove the dough from the mixer bowl to rise (see pages 50–51).

The dough will collect around the hook as it is kneaded

— HANDY TIPS —

• Only use an electric mixer with a proper dough hook for kneading. A mixer with only paddle and whisk attachments is not equipped for breadmaking.

• An electric mixer is particularly helpful for kneading very stiff doughs, as well as doughs with enrichments and flavourings added to them.

• Check the recipe for the dough consistency required. Add extra water, if needed, 1 tablespoon at a time.

RISING & KNOCKING BACK

THE SPEED OF RISING depends on certain factors, such as temperature and humidity, as well as the integral elements of a recipe, such as the type of flour and the method of leavening (that is, with or without a starter). On a warm, humid day dough should rise more quickly than on a cold, dry one; however, the exact effect of temperature can be difficult to predict. Rising times become more predictable only after years of experience with the same bread recipes. The novice baker might find it difficult to tell when the dough has doubled in size; use the test described in step 3 to help check the progress. If the dough over-rises see page 163 for a remedy.

RISING

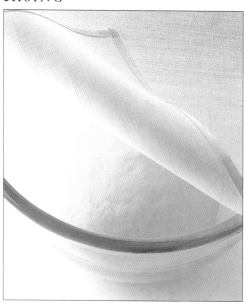

1 Place the kneaded dough in a lightly oiled, glass or ceramic bowl large enough to allow the dough to double in size. Metal containers should be avoided since they can conduct heat, causing the dough to rise too quickly. Cover the bowl with a tea towel and leave to rise in a cool to normal, draught-free room.

RISING THE DOUGH IN THE REFRIGERATOR
This method allows breadmaking to be split into two stages, and is therefore useful for those with busy schedules. Place the dough in a deep, glass bowl that will allow it to expand, brush with oil, and cover tightly with clingfilm. To achieve a complete rise, refrigerate for at least eight hours. After rising, remove it from the refrigerator. Leave it at room temperature for two hours before proceeding to the shaping stage.

2 Leave the dough to rise until doubled in size. For most doughs this will take 1–2 hours. Wholegrain bread doughs and enriched bread doughs will take longer to rise. The slower a dough rises the more chance there is for it to develop flavour and texture. Do not allow the dough to over-rise.

Air bubbles will appear on the surface of a completely risen dough

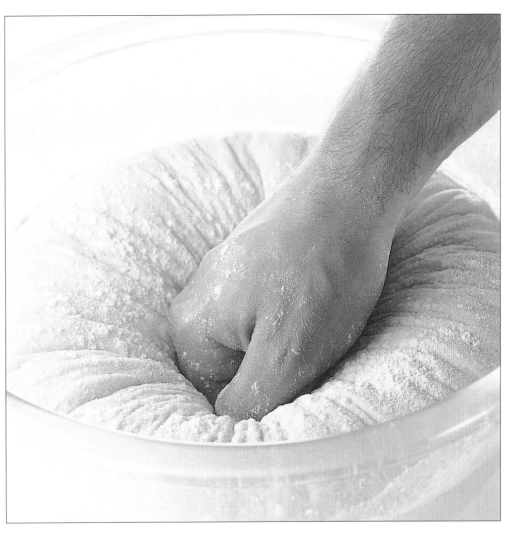

3 To ensure that rising is complete, test the dough by gently pressing with a fingertip. When rising is complete the indentation made will spring back gradually. If the dough is under-risen the indentation will spring back at once. If the dough is over-risen the finger will create a permanent mark that will not spring back at all (*see page 163*).

KNOCKING BACK

ONCE THE DOUGH has risen completely, knock back or deflate the dough by pressing down with your knuckles. Turn the dough out of the bowl on to a lightly floured work surface.

CHAFING

FORM THE DOUGH into a ball by cupping your hands gently around it. Apply a light, downwards pressure to the sides, while simultaneously rotating the dough continuously in a steady, clockwise motion. Continue until the dough is formed into an even, round shape. This action is called chafing. Some recipes specify an extended chafing time at this point. Otherwise, allow the dough to rest for 5 minutes, then proceed to the shaping stage.

Cup the dough gently with your hands

SHAPING & PROVING

AFTER A DOUGH HAS BEEN knocked back and rested, it is ready to be shaped. The techniques on the following six pages illustrate how to form the basic loaf shapes that are most frequently called for in the recipe section. Each stage of the shaping process requires careful attention – handle the dough gently and avoid over-shaping or excessive reshaping. Apply pressure evenly and allow the dough to rest if it begins to resist or tighten. Transfer the shaped loaf to a prepared baking sheet to prove (*see page 57*). Proving allows the dough to rise for a final time before baking. Avoid over-proving the dough; use the recommended test to check its progress.

SHAPING A LONG LOAF

1 Flatten the dough with the lightly floured palm of your hand to expel any gas bubbles. Keep the dough in a round shape by exerting pressure evenly. Take one end of the dough and fold it into the centre. Press gently to seal the fold.

2 Fold the other half of the dough into the centre, so that the two folds overlap along the middle of the loaf. Gently press along the length of the outer seam, using the lightly floured palm of your hand to seal the two folds together.

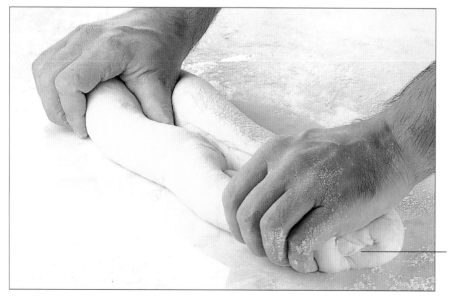

3 Use the thumbs of both hands to create an indentation in the centre of the dough. Before bringing the top half towards you, rest your fingertips along the top of the dough and give a firm, short push forwards. This action tightens the interior of the dough and gives an even-textured crumb when the bread is baked.

Press down into the centre of the dough and fold one half over the other

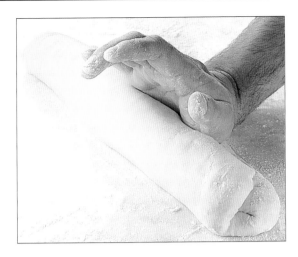

4 Gently press down with the palm of your hand along the seam to seal the fold. Place the dough seam-side down. Press evenly with the palms of both hands and roll the dough backwards and forwards to achieve the desired length as specified in the recipe.

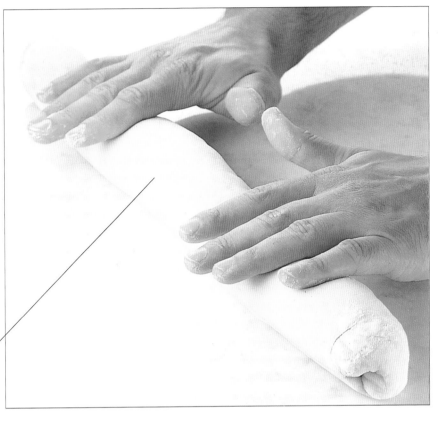

SHAPING A BAGUETTE

TO MAKE A BAGUETTE, shape the dough as for a long loaf following steps 1–4. With your hands placed at either end of the loaf, continue to gently roll the dough backwards and forwards, moving both hands outwards along the loaf. If the dough resists or tightens, allow it to rest for 5 minutes. Repeat the rolling action until an even thickness and the desired length are achieved.

Roll the dough while moving your hands outwards along the loaf

SHAPING DOUGH FOR A LOAF TIN

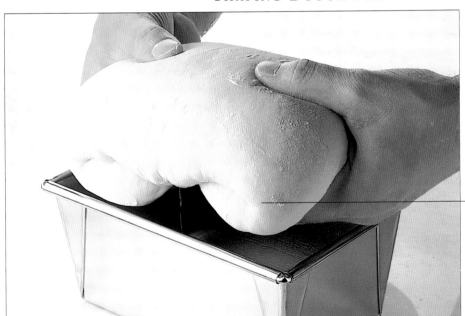

Shape the dough as for a long loaf up to step 3, opposite. Place the dough seam-side down on the work surface. Use the straightened fingers of both hands to gently roll the dough backwards and forwards. Continue until the dough is the same length as the tin and is an even thickness. Lift the dough off the work surface. Tuck under the ends and place the dough into the prepared tin, seam-side down.

Fold the dough to fit the length of the tin

SHAPING A ROUND LOAF

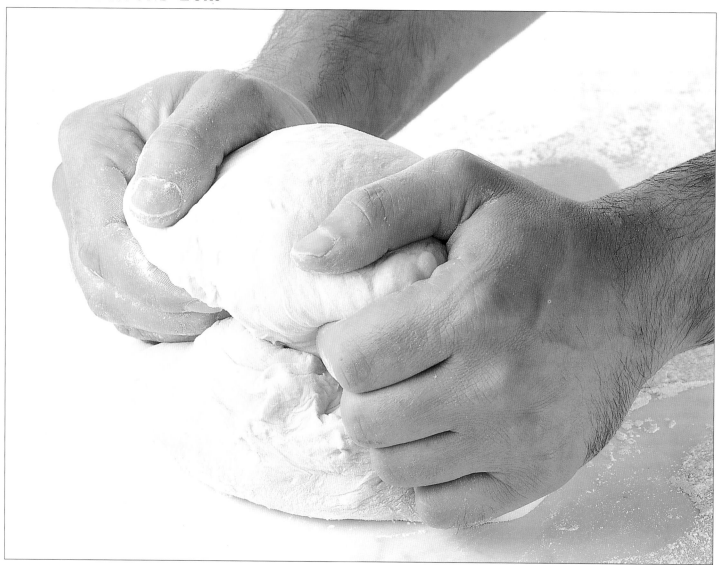

1 Gently press your fingers into the base of the rounded dough (*see page 51*) while holding it with both hands as you would the steering wheel of a car. Rotate the dough between your cupped hands. As the dough is turned, exert light pressure with the tips of your fingers, while at the same time tucking the sides of the dough under what will become the base of the loaf.

2 When the dough becomes smooth and rounded, place the base of the loaf face down on a lightly floured work surface. Cup both hands around the dough and rotate it continuously in a steady, clockwise motion (*see Chafing, page 51*) until a smooth, evenly shaped round is formed. Turn the dough over so that the base is now facing upwards and pinch the seam, or "key", together. Place the loaf "key"-side down on a baking sheet.

APPLYING STEAM TO THE OVEN

STEAM PLAYS AN IMPORTANT ROLE in many bread recipes, especially those that require a crisp, crusty exterior. It is introduced into the oven before and sometimes during baking. The moisture in the air surrounding the bread in the oven affects both its texture and appearance. Moisture helps to soften the crust during the initial stages of baking. This allows the dough to rise fully, and a thin, crisp outer crust to form. Moisture also helps to caramelize the natural sugars in the bread, resulting in a rich, golden brown crust.

USING A SPRAYER

APPLY STEAM WITH A WATER SPRAYER after placing the loaf in the preheated oven. Mist the oven walls eight to ten times, then repeat the process after 2 minutes and again after 2 minutes more. Shut the door rapidly each time to minimize any heat loss from the oven. Be careful to spray only the sides of the oven, avoiding the oven light, electric heating coils, and oven fan.

USING ICE CUBES

APPLY STEAM BY PLACING A WIDE DISH of ice cubes on the bottom rack or floor of the oven while the oven preheats. Place the loaf in the oven before the ice cubes have completely melted. When the ice cubes have melted, carefully remove the dish from the oven. This should occur within the first 15–20 minutes of the bread's baking time.

USING CERAMIC TILES

LINE THE BOTTOM RACK of the oven with unglazed ceramic tiles, leaving 5cm (2in) of air space around the tiles and the oven wall to allow for air circulation. The tiles will produce a steady, radiating heat and help to retain a maximum amount of moisture in the oven. When tiles are used in combination with the applied steam methods and the bread is baked directly on the tiled surface, it will form the crispest crust of the three methods.

BAKING

BAKING IS THE CULMINATION of the breadmaking process, when all of your hard work and patience are rewarded. For a successful loaf follow these simple guidelines: use a good thermometer to regulate the temperature of the oven; preheat to the correct temperature before placing the bread in the oven to bake; make a note of the exact baking time before beginning; and always use a kitchen timer to keep track of the time. An important key to proficient baking lies in knowing your oven and being able to control its temperature closely – each oven is slightly different and has its own peculiarities.

BAKING STAGES

1 When the bread is placed in the hot oven, the heat turns the moisture in the dough to steam, causing the loaf to rise rapidly in the first 20 minutes of baking. The heat then penetrates the bread, killing the active yeast cells and allowing the exterior crust to form.

GETTING TO KNOW YOUR OVEN
Since each oven is different it is difficult to establish hard and fast rules for breadmaking, such as oven shelf position. The only solution is increased familiarity with your oven. Using an oven thermometer before and during baking allows you to observe any variations in temperature and to make adjustments. If you find that you have "hot spots" (uneven heat), in your oven it is important to turn the bread half-way through baking.

2 As the exterior crust forms, the natural sugars in the dough caramelize, creating a golden brown colour. The baking time is specified in each recipe. High humidity, however, can sometimes extend the required baking time and needs to be taken into consideration on the day of baking.

The dough's natural sugars caramelize to give a golden crust

TESTING FOR DONENESS

UNDERCOOKING BREAD is a common mistake of the novice baker. Bread is indigestible when it has been undercooked so it is important to test for doneness. A well-baked bread should be golden brown, not too pale or too dark in colour. The texture and feel of the bread should be firm to the touch without seeming hard. The best test, however, is to listen to the sound of the baked loaf when it is tapped on the underside. It should sound slightly hollow when it has been properly cooked.

COOLING

IT IS IMPORTANT to allow a freshly baked loaf to cool on a wire rack. As the loaf cools, steam from the middle works its way towards the crust, causing it to soften. Cooling baked bread on a wire rack prevents the bottom crust from becoming damp and soggy.

SLICING

WHEN SLICING BREAD use a sharp, serrated bread knife and a clean bread board. Breads should be left to cool slightly before slicing. Use a steady, sawing motion across the top of the bread to prevent the weight of the knife from crushing the loaf or tearing the crust.

USING A BREAD MACHINE

THE MANUFACTURER'S INSTRUCTION MANUAL is an invaluable resource for getting the best results from your machine. A bread machine will mix, knead, rise and bake a loaf. Machine models vary in the shape and the size of loaf they make as well as in how they operate. Some machines have programmable cycles for making different kinds of bread dough, others offer fewer alternatives. A recipe booklet comes with most models. Master a few of these recipes to familiarize yourself with the way your machine works, its possibilities and its limitations. Use the experience to adapt the recipes in this book following the general guidelines given here.

1 Add the ingredients to the baking cylinder in the order suggested in the instruction manual. This will vary depending on the machine model you have. The manufacturer's instructions will tell you what type of yeast to use. The best results are achieved with a yeast made for bread machines; easy-blend yeast also works. Place the baking cylinder inside the machine, select a setting on the control panel, according to the manual, and press start.

HANDY TIPS

• *Pay attention to the order in which the ingredients are added to the machine; it does make a difference.*

• *Keep the lid open to watch the mixing and kneading cycles, but make sure that the lid is shut during rising and baking.*

• *Use the handle of a wooden spoon to remove the kneading paddle from the bottom of the hot, baked loaf.*

RECIPES

OVER 100 BREADS CAN BE CREATED USING THIS RECIPE SECTION. EACH ONE IS A VARIATION ON A VERY SIMPLE THEME: FLOUR, WATER, LEAVENING, AND TIME. BEGIN WITH THE BASIC AND STARTER BREAD RECIPES, WHICH UTILIZE METHODS ILLUSTRATED IN THE BASIC TECHNIQUES. FLAVOURED BREADS PROVIDE AN EXTRA TASTE DIMENSION, WHILE ENRICHED BREADS TRANSFORM BASIC BREAD DOUGH WITH THE ADDITIONS OF OIL, BUTTER, AND EGGS. QUICK, FLAT, AND FESTIVE BREADS OFFER OTHER DELICIOUS POSSIBILITIES FROM AROUND THE WORLD.

  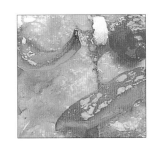

BASIC BREADS

THE RECIPES IN THIS CHAPTER require no advanced skills, only your hands, your attention, and your time. They represent the backbone of the book utilizing the skills covered in the Basic Techniques section (*see pages 38–69*). Read this section first and you will be able to tackle all of the basic bread recipes with ease and confidence. These simple breads give the novice baker the opportunity to experiment, to observe the transformation of the ingredients into bread, and to gain valuable experience. Later in the recipe section other elements, such as starters, flavourings, and enrichments are added to the basic ingredients of flour, water, and yeast. These additions introduce the baker to new techniques and skills illustrated with the recipes.

PAIN ORDINAIRE
PLAIN OR BASIC WHITE BREAD

Treat this recipe as a blueprint for the basic method of breadmaking. A wide variety of breads can be created using this simple dough recipe. For a more rustic flavour, substitute 125g (4oz) of wholemeal, rye, or barley flour for the same amount of strong white flour. For an extra-tender crumb, substitute 175ml (6fl oz) of the water for the same amount of yogurt or buttermilk and add it to the well in step 3.

INGREDIENTS
2 tsp dried yeast
350ml (12fl oz) water
500g (1lb) strong white flour
1½ tsp salt

1 Sprinkle the yeast into 100ml (3½fl oz) of the water in a bowl. Leave for 5 minutes; stir to dissolve. Mix the flour and salt together in a large bowl. Make a well in the centre and pour in the yeasted water.

2 Use a wooden spoon to draw enough of the flour into the yeasted water to form a soft paste. Cover the bowl with a tea towel and leave the paste to "sponge" until frothy, loose, and slightly expanded, about 20 minutes.

3 Pour the remaining water, holding back about half, into the centre of the well. Mix in the flour from the sides of the well. Stir in the reserved water, as needed, to form a firm, moist dough.

4 Turn the dough out on to a lightly floured work surface. Knead until smooth, shiny, and elastic, about 10 minutes.

5 Put the dough in a clean bowl and cover with a tea towel. Leave to rise until doubled in size, about 1½–2 hours.

6 Knock back, then leave to rest for 10 minutes. Shape the dough into a long loaf (*see pages 52–53*), about 35cm (14in) in length. Place the shaped loaf on a floured baking sheet and cover with a tea towel. Prove until doubled in size, about 45 minutes.

7 Cut five diagonal slashes (*see page 62*), each about 5mm (¼in) deep, across the top of the loaf. Bake in the preheated oven for 45 minutes until golden brown and hollow-sounding when tapped underneath. Leave the baked bread to cool on a wire rack.

 To begin
Sponge method
Time: 20 minutes
(*see page 44*)

 Rising
1½–2 hours
(*see pages 50–51*)

 Proving
45 minutes
(*see page 57*)

 Oven temperature
220°C/425°F/gas 7

 Baking
45 minutes
Steam optional
(*see page 63*)

 Yield
1 loaf

 Yeast alternative
15g (½oz) fresh yeast
(*see page 41*)

CLASSIC PAIN ORDINAIRE

SHAPING A COTTAGE LOAF

Divide the dough into two-thirds and a third. Shape each piece into a round loaf (see pages 54–55). Place the small loaf on top of the large loaf. Plunge two fingers into the centres of the stacked loaves to join them together.

VARIATIONS

Cottage Loaf

• Make one quantity Pain Ordinaire dough up to step 6.
• Shape the bread dough into a cottage loaf shape (*see left*).
• Place on a floured baking sheet and cover with a tea towel. Prove until doubled in size, about 45 minutes. Preheat the oven to 220°C/425°F/gas 7. Sift over a dusting of flour.
• Bake for 45 minutes, as directed in step 7. Cool on a wire rack.

Petits Pains (Bread Rolls)

• Make one quantity Pain Ordinaire dough up to step 6.
• Divide the bread dough into eight pieces and shape into smooth, round rolls (*see page 55*).
• Place on a floured baking sheet and cover with a tea towel. Prove until doubled in size, about 30 minutes. Preheat the oven to 220°C/425°F/gas 7.
• Sift over a light dusting of flour. Use a pair of scissors to snip an "X" in the centre of each roll (*see page 62*).

• Bake for 25 minutes until hollow-sounding when tapped underneath. Leave to cool on a wire rack.

Granary Tin Loaf

• Make one quantity Pain Ordinaire dough up to step 6, replacing the strong white flour with the same amount of granary flour in step 1.
• Grease a 500g (1lb) loaf tin with oil. Shape the dough for a loaf tin (*see page 53*) and place the dough in the tin, seam-side down.
• Cover with a tea towel and prove until the dough is 1cm (½in) below the top of the tin, about 30 minutes.
• If desired, cut a lengthways slash (*see page 62*) for a split tin loaf. Leave the dough to rise further until it is 1cm (½in) above the top of the tin, about 15 minutes. Preheat the oven to 220°C/425°F/gas 7.
• Brush the top with water and bake for 20 minutes. Reduce the oven to 200°C/400°F/gas 6 and bake for a further 15–20 minutes, until hollow-sounding when tapped. Turn out on to a wire rack and leave to cool.

— HANDY TIPS —

• *Use tepid water to dissolve the yeast (see page 41). Tepid water should be comfortable to the touch, not too hot, but not too cool.*

• *It is important that the dough is soft and not too dry before it is kneaded. Add more water 1 tablespoon at a time, as needed, to achieve a consistency indicated in the recipe.*

• *When kneading the dough use extra flour sparingly. Work the dough slowly and firmly; it will gradually become more elastic and easier to knead.*

USING A BREAD MACHINE

Use the dough setting (see pages 66–67). Remove the dough after rising and follow steps 6 and 7.

COTTAGE LOAF

GRANARY TIN LOAF

PETITS PAINS

COUNTRY OATMEAL BREAD

Sometimes called Monastery bread, this coarse, crunchy British bread originated in northern England. It is best eaten for breakfast or afternoon tea, thickly spread with yellow, salted butter and fragrant, creamy honey, or try it with a chunk of Cheddar cheese and a mug of ale.

USING A BREAD MACHINE

Use the dough setting (see pages 66–67). Remove the dough after rising and follow steps 5 and 6.

INGREDIENTS

2 tsp dried yeast

350ml (12fl oz) water

250g (8oz) wholemeal flour

125g (4oz) strong white flour

125g (4oz) medium oatmeal

1½ tsp salt

1 tsp runny honey

rolled oats, for topping

1 Sprinkle the yeast into 100ml (3½fl oz) of the water in a bowl. Leave for 5 minutes; stir to dissolve. Mix the flours, oatmeal, and salt together in a large bowl. Make a well in the centre and pour in the yeasted water and runny honey.

2 Pour the remaining water, holding back about half, into the well. Mix in the flour, then stir in the reserved water, as needed, to form a stiff, sticky dough.

3 Turn the dough out on to a work surface lightly sprinkled with oatmeal. Knead until smooth and elastic, about 10 minutes.

4 Put the dough in a clean bowl and cover with a tea towel. Leave to rise until doubled in size, about 1½–2 hours.

5 Knock back, then leave to rest for 10 minutes. Grease a 500g (1lb) loaf tin. Shape the dough for a loaf tin (*see page 53*). Place the dough in the tin, seam-side down. Cover with a tea towel and prove until doubled in size, about 1 hour.

6 Brush the loaf lightly with water and sprinkle with rolled oats over the top. Bake in the preheated oven for 1 hour until golden brown and hollow-sounding when tapped underneath. Turn out of the tin and leave to cool on a wire rack.

VARIATIONS
Barley Bread

• Make one quantity Country Oatmeal Bread dough. Replace the flours with 250g (8oz) strong white flour, 125g (4oz) barley flour, and 125g (4oz) wholemeal flour. Follow the recipe up to step 6. Preheat the oven to 200°C/400°F/gas 6.
• Brush the loaf lightly with water and sprinkle with barley flakes instead of the rolled oats in step 6.
• Bake for 1 hour until golden brown and hollow-sounding when tapped underneath. Turn out and leave to cool on a wire rack.

Oatmeal Rolls

• Make one quantity Country Oatmeal Bread dough up to step 4.
• Divide the dough into 16 equal pieces and shape into smooth, round rolls (*see page 55*). Place the rolls on two greased baking sheets. Cover with a tea towel and prove until doubled in size, about 30–45 minutes. Preheat the oven to 200°C/400°F/gas 6.
• Brush the rolls lightly with water and sprinkle with rolled oats.
• Bake for 20–30 minutes until golden and hollow-sounding when tapped underneath. Leave to cool on a wire rack.

 Rising
1½–2 hours
(*see pages 50–51*)

 Proving
1 hour
(*see page 57*)

 Oven temperature
200°C/400°F/gas 6

 Baking
1 hour
Steam optional
(*see page 63*)

 Yield
1 loaf

 Yeast alternative
15g (½oz)
fresh yeast
(*see page 41*)

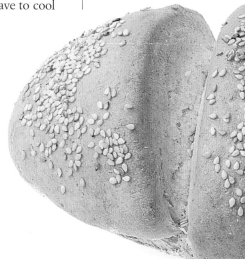

DAKTYLA
GREEK VILLAGE BREAD

This sesame seed-coated bread is traditionally made with "yellow" or "country" flour, a blend of white and wholemeal flour mixed with finely ground cornmeal. Alternatively, it can be made just with strong white flour. In Greece, the bread is commonly known as Daktyla, *meaning "fingers", because it is broken into fingers of bread to eat.*

USING A BREAD MACHINE
Use the dough setting (see pages 66–67). Remove the dough after rising and follow steps 6 and 7.

INGREDIENTS

2 tsp dried yeast

350ml (12fl oz) water

350g (12oz) strong white flour

75g (2½oz) wholemeal flour

75g (2½oz) fine cornmeal

1 tsp salt

1 tbsp olive oil

1 tbsp runny honey

1 tbsp milk, plus extra to glaze

sesame seeds, to decorate

1 Sprinkle the yeast into 100ml (3½fl oz) of the water in a bowl. Leave for 5 minutes; stir to dissolve. Mix the flours, cornmeal, and salt together thoroughly in a large bowl. Make a well in the centre and pour in the yeasted water.

2 Use a wooden spoon to draw enough of the flour into the yeasted water to form a soft paste. Cover the bowl with a tea towel, then leave to "sponge" until frothy and risen, 20 minutes. Add the oil, honey, and milk to the sponge.

3 Pour the remaining water, holding back about half, into the well. Mix in the flour. Stir in the reserved liquid, as needed, to form a firm, moist dough.

4 Turn the dough out on to a lightly floured work surface. Knead until smooth, shiny, and elastic, about 10 minutes.

5 Put the dough in a clean bowl and cover with a tea towel. Leave to rise until doubled in size, about 1½ hours.

6 Knock back, leave to rest for 10 minutes. Divide the dough into six pieces. Shape each piece into an oblong, then arrange in a row, just touching, on a floured baking sheet. Cover with a tea towel and prove until doubled in size, about 1 hour.

7 Brush the top of the loaf with milk and sprinkle with the sesame seeds. Bake in the preheated oven for 45 minutes until hollow-sounding when tapped underneath. Leave to cool on a wire rack.

To begin
Sponge method
Time: 20 minutes
(*see page 44*)

Rising
1½ hours
(*see pages 50–51*)

Proving
1 hour
(*see page 57*)

Oven temperature
220°C/425°F/gas 7

Baking
45 minutes
Steam optional
(*see page 63*)

Yield
1 loaf

Yeast alternative
15g (½oz)
fresh yeast
(*see page 41*)

VICTORIAN MILK BREAD

This is a bread with a soft crust and crumb, which keeps well and makes crisp, nutty toast. It is a very good dough for making a decorative plait (see page 57).

(see page 57)

USING A BREAD MACHINE

Use the dough setting (see pages 66–67). Remove the dough after rising and follow steps 5 and 6.

INGREDIENTS

2 tsp dried yeast

1 tsp granulated sugar

350ml (12fl oz) tepid milk

500g (1lb) strong white flour

1½ tsp salt

egg glaze, made with 1 egg and 1 tbsp milk (see page 58)

1 Sprinkle the yeast and sugar into 100ml (3½fl oz) of milk in a bowl. Leave for 5 minutes; stir to dissolve. Stir in half of the remaining milk.

2 Mix the flour and salt together in a large bowl. Make a well in the centre and pour in the yeasted milk. Mix in the flour. Stir in the reserved milk to form a sticky dough.

3 Turn the dough out on to a lightly floured work surface. Knead the dough until smooth and elastic, about 10 minutes.

4 Put the dough in a clean bowl and cover with a tea towel. Leave to rise for 45 minutes.

5 Knock back, cover, and leave the dough to rise again until doubled in size, about 45 minutes. Grease a 500g (1lb) loaf tin. Shape the dough into an S-shape to fit in a loaf tin (*see right*). Cover with a tea towel, then prove until the dough is 2.5cm (1in) above the top of the tin, about 1 hour.

6 Brush the top of the loaf with the egg glaze. Bake in the preheated oven for 45 minutes until golden and hollow-sounding when tapped underneath. Turn out on to a wire rack and leave to cool.

VARIATION
Bloomer
(see page 16 for illustration)
• Make one quantity Victorian Milk Bread dough, replacing half the milk with water, up to step 4.
• Leave to rise for 2 hours. Knock back and leave to rest for 5 minutes.
• Shape into a long loaf, about 25cm (10in) in length and 12.5cm (5in) wide (*see pages 52–53*). Prove as directed, about 1 hour.
• Cut five deep slashes across the top of the loaf (*see page 62*). Preheat the oven to 220°C/425°F/gas 7.
• Sift over a fine layer of flour. Bake as directed in step 6.

 Rising
1½ hours
(see pages 50–51)

 Proving
1 hour
(see page 57)

 Oven temperature
200°C/400°F/gas 6

 Baking
45 minutes

 Yield
1 loaf

Yeast alternative
15g (½oz) fresh yeast
(see page 41)

SHAPING THE DOUGH

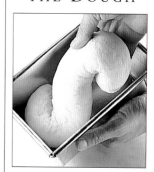

Shape the dough into a long loaf (see pages 52–53), about 40cm (16in) in length and 7.5cm (3¼in) wide. Turn the shaped dough over at each end to form an S-shape. Place the dough in the greased loaf tin. Continue as directed in step 5.

SCOTS BAPS

Scots Baps are best eaten warm, straight from the oven. They are a special treat at breakfast when filled with grilled bacon rashers and a fried egg. The mixture of milk and water gives the rolls a tender crumb and the extra dusting of flour gives them a soft crust.

USING A BREAD MACHINE

Use the dough setting (see pages 66–67). Remove the dough after rising and follow steps 5–8.

INGREDIENTS

175ml (6fl oz) tepid milk

175ml (6fl oz) water

2 tsp dried yeast

1 tsp granulated sugar

500g (1lb) strong white flour

1½ tsp salt

1 tbsp milk, to glaze

1 Combine the milk and water in a liquid measuring jug. Sprinkle the yeast and sugar into 100ml (3½fl oz) of the milk and water mixture in a separate bowl. Leave for 5 minutes; stir to dissolve. Stir in half of the remaining milk and water mixture.

2 Mix the flour and salt together in a large bowl. Make a well in the centre and pour in the yeasted milk and water. Mix in the flour. Stir in the reserved milk and water, as needed, to form a sticky dough.

3 Turn the dough out on to a lightly floured work surface. Knead the dough until smooth and elastic, about 10 minutes.

4 Put the dough in a clean bowl and cover with a tea towel. Leave to rise until doubled in size, about 1 hour.

5 Knock back, leave to rest for 10 minutes. Divide into eight pieces. Shape each one into a flat oval, about 1cm (½in) thick. Put on a floured baking sheet. Brush with milk and sift over a heavy dusting of flour.

6 Leave to prove, uncovered, until doubled in size, 30–45 minutes.

7 Sift a heavy dusting of flour again over each bap. Use your thumb to make an impression in the centre of each bap, about 1cm (½in) deep.

8 Bake in the preheated oven for 15–20 minutes until risen and pale golden. Cover with a tea towel and leave to cool on a wire rack.

VARIATION
Kentish Huffkins

• Make one quantity Scots Baps dough up to step 4.

• Divide the dough into 12 equal pieces. Shape each piece of dough into a round ball (*see page 55*). Place on a floured baking sheet.

• Use a floured finger to form a deep indentation in the centre of each roll. Prove until doubled in size, 30–45 minutes. Preheat the oven to 200°C/400°F/gas 6.

• Bake as directed in step 8. Leave to cool on a wire rack. Fill the indent with jam and cream to serve.

 Rising
1 hour
(*see pages 50–51*)

 Proving
30–45 minutes
(*see page 57*)

 Oven temperature
200°C/400°F/gas 6

 Baking
15–20 minutes

 Yield
8 baps

 Yeast alternative
15g (½oz)
fresh yeast
(*see page 41*)

BALLYMALOE BROWN BREAD

This no-knead bread revolutionized English women's lives in the 1940s when it was introduced by Doris Grant in her book Your Daily Bread. This improved version was devised by Myrtle Allen, founder of Ballymaloe House hotel and cookery school in County Cork, Ireland.

USING A BREAD MACHINE

This bread may be made entirely in a machine. Follow the manufacturer's instructions (see pages 66–67).

INGREDIENTS

3½ tsp dried yeast

400ml (14fl oz) water

1 tsp black treacle or molasses

500g (1lb) wholemeal flour

2 tsp salt

1 Grease a 500g (1lb) loaf tin and warm it in a preheated oven, 120°C/250°F/gas ½ for 10 minutes.

2 Sprinkle the yeast into 150ml (¼ pint) of the water in a bowl. Leave for 5 minutes; stir to dissolve. Add the treacle or molasses. Leave for a further 10 minutes until frothy. Add the remaining water and stir.

3 Mix the flour and salt together in a large bowl. Make a well in the centre and pour in the yeasted mixture. Stir in the flour from the sides to form a thick batter.

4 Use your hands to mix the batter gently in the bowl for 1 minute until it begins to leave the sides of the bowl clean, and forms into a soft, sticky dough.

5 Place the dough in the prepared tin and cover with a tea towel. Leave to prove until the dough is 1cm (½in) above the top of the tin, about 25–30 minutes.

6 Bake in the preheated oven at 220°C/425°F/gas 7 for 30 minutes, then lower the temperature to 200°C/400°F/gas 6 and bake for a further 15 minutes.

7 Turn the loaf out on to a baking sheet. Return the bread, bottom-side up, to the oven. Bake for a further 10 minutes until golden and hollow-sounding when tapped underneath. Cool on a wire rack.

 Proving
25–30 minutes
(see page 57)

 Oven temperature
220°C/425°F/gas 7

 Baking
55 minutes

 Yield
1 loaf

 Yeast alternative
30g (1oz)
fresh yeast
(see page 41)

BROA

PORTUGUESE CORN BREAD

This famous yellow cornmeal bread originated in the Minho province in northern Portugal. It is eaten traditionally with Caldo Verde, Portugal's famous kale and sausage soup. (See page 19 for an illustration of the bread.)

USING A BREAD MACHINE

Use the dough setting (see pages 66–67). Remove the dough after rising and follow steps 5 and 6.

INGREDIENTS

2 tsp dried yeast

150ml (¼ pint) tepid milk

200ml (7fl oz) water

200g (7oz) yellow cornmeal

300g (10oz) strong white flour, sifted

1½ tsp salt

1 tbsp olive oil

1 Sprinkle the yeast into the milk in a bowl. Leave for 5 minutes; stir with a wooden spoon. Add the water to the milk. Mix the cornmeal, flour, and salt in a large bowl. Make a well in the centre and pour in the yeasted liquid and olive oil.

2 Mix in the flour to form a firm and moist, but not sticky, dough that leaves the sides of the bowl.

3 Turn the dough out on to a lightly floured work surface. Knead the dough until smooth and elastic, about 10 minutes.

4 Put the dough in a clean bowl and cover with a tea towel. Leave to rise until doubled in size, about 1½ hours.

5 Knock back, leave to rest for 10 minutes. Shape into a round loaf (see page 54). Place on a baking sheet sprinkled with corn-meal and cover with a tea towel. Prove until doubled in size, about 1 hour.

6 Dust the loaf with cornmeal. Bake in the preheated oven for 45 minutes until golden and hollow-sounding when tapped underneath. Leave to cool on a wire rack.

 Rising
1½ hours
(see pages 50–51)

 Proving
1 hour
(see page 57)

 Oven temperature
200°C/400°F/gas 6

 Baking
45 minutes
Steam optional
(see page 63)

 Yield
1 loaf

 Yeast alternative
15g (½oz)
fresh yeast
(see page 41)

LANDBROT
GERMAN COUNTRY-STYLE RYE BREAD

Rye was traditionally the most important of all grain crops to Germany, and German bakers remain the undisputed masters of rye breads. Landbrot translates literally as "bread of the land", and it is the German equivalent of Pain de Campagne. It is baked throughout Germany, and although there are regional differences in colour and texture, because the proportions of rye to wheat vary, it is usually dusted with flour. (See page 18 for an illustration of the bread.)

USING A BREAD MACHINE
This recipe is not suitable for bread machines.

INGREDIENTS
for the starter

½ tsp dried yeast

3 tbsp water

50g (1¾oz) strong white flour

1 tbsp milk

for the dough

1½ tsp dried yeast

350ml (12fl oz) water

350g (12oz) rye flour

100g (3½oz) strong white flour

2 tsp salt

1 **To make the starter** Sprinkle the yeast into the water in a bowl. Leave for 5 minutes; stir to dissolve. Mix in the flour and milk. Cover with a tea towel and leave to ferment at room temperature for 12–18 hours. The mixture will be bubbly and pleasantly sour-smelling.

2 **To make the dough** Sprinkle the yeast into 250ml (8fl oz) of the water in a bowl. Leave for 5 minutes; stir to dissolve. Mix the flours together in a large bowl. Make a well in the centre and add the yeasted water and starter.

3 Use a wooden spoon to draw enough of the flour into the starter mixture to form a thick batter. Cover the bowl with a tea towel and leave to "sponge" until frothy and risen, 12–18 hours.

4 Add the salt to the fermented batter, then mix in the flour. Stir in the reserved water, as needed, to form a stiff, sticky dough.

5 Turn the dough out on to a lightly floured work surface. Knead until smooth and elastic, about 10 minutes. Leave to rest for a further 10 minutes.

6 Shape the dough into a round loaf (*see page 54*). Place on a floured baking sheet. Dust the loaf with flour. Cut one slash, 1cm (½in) deep, across the top of the loaf, then another in the opposite direction to make an "X" (*see page 62*).

7 Cover with a tea towel and prove until doubled in size, about 1½ hours.

8 Bake in the preheated oven for 1¼ hours until hollow-sounding when tapped underneath. Leave to cool on a wire rack.

VARIATIONS
Seeded German Rye Bread
• Combine 2 tablespoons each linseeds, sesame seeds, and pumpkin seeds in a food processor. Using the pulse button process until roughly chopped. Alternatively, grind by hand using a pestle and mortar.
• Make one quantity Landbrot dough up to step 4.
• Add the seed mixture with the salt to the fermented batter. Continue as directed in steps 4–5.
• Shape the dough for a greased 1kg (2lb) loaf tin (*see page 53*).
• Prove as directed in step 7. Preheat the oven to 200°C/400°F/gas 6.
• Brush with milk and sprinkle with whole linseeds, sesame seeds, and pumpkin seeds.
• Bake as directed in step 8.

Rye Bread with Caraway Seeds
• Make one quantity Landbrot dough adding ½ teaspoon caraway seeds to the starter in step 1.
• Shape the dough for a greased 1kg (2lb) loaf tin (*see page 53*).
• Prove as directed in step 7. Preheat the oven to 200°C/400°F/gas 6.
• Brush with milk and sprinkle evenly with 2 tablespoons rye flakes over the top of the loaf.
• Bake as directed in step 8.

To begin
Starter
Time: 12–18 hours
(*see page 42*)

Sponge method
Time: 12–18 hours
(*see page 44*)

Proving
1½ hours
(*see page 57*)

Oven temperature
200°C/400°F/gas 6

Baking
1¼ hours
Steam optional
(*see page 63*)

Yield
1 loaf

Yeast alternative
For the starter:
2.5g (⅛oz)
fresh yeast
For the dough:
10g (⅓oz)
fresh yeast
(*see page 41*)

PAIN DE SEIGLE
FRENCH RYE BREAD

In France, rye bread originated in mountainous regions, such as the Alps, Pyrenees, and Vosges, where it was a staple, everyday bread. Today, rye bread is eaten more infrequently, but it is always served, thinly sliced and thickly buttered, as an accompaniment to oysters or the gargantuan plateau de fruits de mer, which is a speciality of the brasseries of Paris.

USING A BREAD MACHINE
This recipe is not suitable for bread machines.

INGREDIENTS
for the starter
2 tsp dried yeast

150ml (¼ pint) water

125g (4oz) strong white flour

for the dough
75g (2½oz) strong white flour

300g (10oz) rye flour

2 tsp salt

250ml (8fl oz) water

1 To make the starter Sprinkle the yeast into the water in a bowl. Leave for 5 minutes; stir to dissolve. Add the flour and mix to form a thick batter. Cover with a tea towel and leave for 2 hours.

2 To make the dough Mix the flours and the salt together in a large bowl. Make a well in the centre and pour in the starter and half of the water.

3 Mix in the flour. Stir in the remaining water to form a fairly moist, sticky dough.

4 Turn the dough out on to a lightly floured work surface. Knead the dough until smooth and elastic, about 10 minutes.

5 Put the dough in a clean bowl and cover with a tea towel. Leave to rise until doubled in size, about 1 hour. Knock back, then leave to rest for 10 minutes.

6 Divide the dough into two pieces and shape each piece into a long loaf (*see pages 52–53*), about 30cm (12in) in length. Place the loaves on a floured baking sheet and leave to rest for 5 minutes.

7 Lightly dust the loaves with flour. Cut six or seven short, parallel slashes, 5mm (¼in) deep, at 1cm (½in) intervals, down both sides of the loaves (*see page 62*). Cover with a tea towel and prove until doubled in size, about 1½ hours.

8 Bake in the preheated oven for 45 minutes until hollow-sounding when tapped underneath. Leave to cool on a wire rack.

To begin
Starter
Time: 2 hours
(*see page 42*)

Rising
1 hour
(*see pages 50–51*)

Proving
1½ hours
(*see page 57*)

Oven temperature
200°C/400°F/gas 6

Baking
45 minutes
Steam optional
(*see page 63*)

Yield
2 small loaves

Yeast alternative
15g (½oz)
fresh yeast
(*see page 41*)

ENRICHED
BREADS

THE ADDITION OF ONE OR MORE ENRICHING INGREDIENTS – SUCH AS BUTTER, OIL, OR EGGS – RESULTS IN A BREAD WITH A SOFT, TENDER CRUMB THAT BECOMES MORE CAKE-LIKE IN DIRECT PROPORTION TO THE QUANTITIES OF THE ENRICHMENTS ADDED. THE MOISTURE IN THESE INGREDIENTS MAKES THE DOUGH SOFT AND OFTEN DIFFICULT TO HANDLE. THE FAT IN THEM COATS THE GLUTEN STRANDS IN THE DOUGH AND CREATES A BARRIER BETWEEN THE FLOUR AND THE YEAST. THIS LENGTHENS THE RISING TIMES SO MUCH THAT IN BREADS LIKE BRIOCHE, THE ENRICHMENTS ARE ADDED AFTER AN INITIAL RISING. THE RECIPES IN THIS SECTION MAY REQUIRE SOME NEW SKILLS AND A BIT MORE CONFIDENCE AND TIME THAN PREVIOUS RECIPES, BUT THEY ARE WORTH IT.

LEFT **AN INDIVIDUAL BRIOCHE AND THE LARGER BRIOCHE A TETE**

BRIOCHE

Egg-and-butter enriched Brioche *dough is formed into a variety of shapes, but perhaps the classic and most characteristic is that of the small* Brioche Parisienne, *with its distinctive topknot and scalloped underside. Perhaps best enjoyed at breakfast with raspberry conserve and a steaming bowl of* café au lait, *the culinary status of* Brioche *far outstrips the breakfast table.* Brioche *dough is favoured above other doughs and pastries in some celebrated classic dishes, most notably Beef Wellington.*

USING A BREAD MACHINE

This bread may be made in a machine which has a double-rising setting (check the manufacturer's instructions). Either make it entirely in the machine or remove the dough after the second kneading and follow steps 7–10.

INGREDIENTS

2½ tsp dried yeast

2 tbsp water

375g (13oz) strong white flour

2 tbsp granulated sugar

1½ tsp salt

5 eggs, beaten

15g (½oz) unsalted butter, melted

175g (6oz) unsalted butter, softened, plus extra to brush moulds

egg glaze, made with 1 egg yolk and 1 tbsp water (see page 58)

1 Sprinkle the yeast into the water in a bowl. Leave for 5 minutes; stir to dissolve. Mix the flour, sugar, and salt together in a large bowl.

2 Make a well in the centre and add the yeasted water and beaten eggs (*see below, left*). Mix in the flour to form a soft, moist but manageable dough.

3 Turn the dough out on to a lightly floured work surface. Knead until elastic, about 10 minutes.

4 Grease a large bowl with the melted butter. Place the dough in the bowl; turn it to coat evenly. Cover with a tea towel and leave to rise until doubled in size, about 1–1½ hours. Knock back, then leave to rest for 10 minutes.

5 Use your hand to incorporate the softened butter into the dough (*see below, right*).

6 Turn out on to a lightly floured work surface. Knead until the butter is distributed throughout, 5 minutes, then rest for 5 minutes more. Grease ten brioche moulds, each about 8cm (3½in) in diameter and 5cm (2in) deep, with the extra softened butter (*see opposite, left*).

7 Divide the dough into ten pieces. Pinch off about a quarter of each piece. Use cupped hands to roll both the large and small pieces of dough into smooth, round balls (*see page 55*). Place one of the large balls in each of the prepared brioche moulds.

8 Use your forefinger to make an indentation in the centre of the large ball, then add the small ball (*see opposite, right*). Repeat this step with the remaining balls of dough.

9 Cover the moulds with a tea towel and prove until the dough has doubled in size, 30 minutes.

10 Brush the tops with the egg glaze. Place the moulds on a baking tray and bake in the preheated oven for 15–20 minutes until glossy and golden. Turn out and leave to cool on a wire rack.

 Rising 1–1½ hours (*see pages 50–51*)

 Proving 30 minutes (*see page 57*)

 Oven temperature 220°C/425°F/gas 7

 Baking 15–20 minutes

 Yield 10 small Brioche

 Yeast alternative 20g (¾oz) fresh yeast (*see page 41*)

ADDING ENRICHMENTS TO DOUGH

In step 2, add beaten eggs directly to the flour well along with the yeasted water. Mix in the flour to form a soft, moist but manageable dough.

In step 5, use your hand to squeeze the softened butter into the dough until evenly distributed throughout.

CINNAMON RAISIN BREAD

When sliced and toasted this bread is perhaps North America's favourite breakfast loaf – a great accompaniment to a full weekend breakfast of eggs, bacon, and freshly squeezed juice. Any leftover slices make the perfect ingredients for another weekend breakfast favourite – "French Toast" or Pain Perdu (see page 158).

USING A BREAD MACHINE
Use the dough setting (see pages 66–67). Remove the dough after rising and follow steps 6–9.

INGREDIENTS

90g (3oz) dark brown sugar

200ml (7fl oz) milk

2 tsp dried yeast

500g (1lb) strong white flour

1½ tsp salt

2 tsp ground cinnamon

2 eggs, beaten

3 tbsp unsalted butter, melted

150g (5oz) raisins

egg glaze, made with 1 egg yolk and 1 tbsp water (see page 58)

1 Add the dark brown sugar to 100ml (3½fl oz) of the milk in a bowl. Stir to dissolve completely. Sprinkle the yeast into the milk. Leave for 5 minutes; stir to dissolve.

2 Mix the flour, salt, and cinnamon together in a large bowl. Make a well in the centre and add the yeasted milk, beaten eggs, and melted butter.

3 Mix in the flour. Stir in the remaining milk, as needed, to form a moist, sticky dough.

4 Turn the dough out on to a lightly floured work surface. Knead until smooth, soft, and supple, about 10 minutes.

5 Put the dough in a clean bowl and cover with a tea towel. Leave the dough to rise until doubled in size, about 1–1½ hours.

6 Grease a 1kg (2lb) loaf tin with butter. Knock back the dough, then leave to rest for 10 minutes.

7 Roll out the dough on a lightly floured work surface to form a 20cm x 30cm (8in x 12in) rectangle. Sprinkle with the raisins, pressing them down lightly into the dough.

8 Roll the dough tightly like a Swiss roll. Pinch the seam to seal. Place in the loaf tin with the seam underneath (*see page 53*). Cover with a tea towel and leave to prove until the dough is 1cm (½in) above the top of the tin, 30–45 minutes.

9 Brush the loaf with the egg glaze and bake in the preheated oven for 45 minutes, then reduce the temperature to 180°C/350°F/gas 4 and bake for a further 30 minutes until dark, shiny, and hollow-sounding when tapped underneath. Turn out on to a wire rack and leave to cool.

 Rising
1–1½ hours
(*see pages 50–51*)

 Proving
30–45 minutes
(*see page 57*)

 Oven temperature
200°C/400°F/gas 6

 Baking
1¼ hours

 Yield
1 loaf

Yeast alternative
15g (½oz)
fresh yeast
(*see page 41*)

PRUNE & CHOCOLATE BREAD

INGREDIENTS

2½ tsp dried yeast

350ml (12fl oz) water

500g (1lb) strong white flour

1½ tsp salt

30g (1oz) unsalted butter, softened, plus extra to grease tin

200g (7oz) pitted prunes, roughly chopped

200g (7oz) plain chocolate, roughly chopped

1 egg, beaten

This deeply indulgent loaf, chock-a-block with juicy prunes and melted chocolate, is superlative served warm and cut into thick slices. The prunes and chocolate are best roughly chopped so that the bread is packed with large chunks of flavour. Try the Triple Chocolate and Hazelnut variation as a special treat for your favourite chocolate-lover.

USING A BREAD MACHINE

Use the dough setting (see page 66–67). Remove the dough after rising and follow steps 5–7.

1 Sprinkle the yeast into 100ml (3½fl oz) of the water in a bowl. Leave for 5 minutes, then stir to dissolve. Mix the flour and salt together in a large bowl. Make a well in the centre of the flour and pour in the yeasted water.

2 Mix in the flour. Stir in the remaining water, as needed, to form a soft, sticky dough.

3 Turn the dough out on to a lightly floured work surface. Knead the dough until smooth and elastic, about 10 minutes.

4 Put the dough in a clean bowl and cover with a tea towel. Leave to rise until doubled in size, about 1 hour. Grease a 1kg (2lb) loaf tin with softened butter.

5 Knock back the dough, then leave to rest for 10 minutes. Add the prunes, chocolate, butter, and egg (*see below, left*). Turn out on to a lightly floured work surface. Knead until just firm enough to shape, 1–2 minutes.

6 Shape the dough for a loaf tin (*see below, right*) and place in the prepared tin. Cover with a tea towel and leave to prove until the dough has risen 2.5cm (1in) above the rim of the tin, about 30 minutes.

7 Bake in the preheated oven for 45 minutes until lightly browned and hollow-sounding when tapped underneath. Turn out on to a wire rack and leave to cool.

VARIATION
Triple Chocolate and Hazelnut Bread

• Make one quantity Prune and Chocolate Bread dough up to step 5.
• Replace the prunes and 200g (7oz) plain chocolate in step 5 with: 250g (8oz) plain chocolate, 125g (4oz) dark chocolate, 60g (2oz) milk chocolate, roughly chopped, and 125g (4oz) hazelnuts, toasted and roughly chopped. Add to the dough (*see below, left*).
• Shape, prove, and bake the dough as directed in steps 6 and 7.

Rising
1 hours
(*see pages 50–51*)

Proving
30 minutes
(*see page 57*)

Oven temperature
180°C/350°F/gas 4

Baking
45 minutes

Yield
1 loaf

Yeast alternative
20g (¾oz) fresh yeast
(*see page 41*)

ENRICHING THE DOUGH

Use your hand to gently squeeze the prunes, chocolate, butter, and egg into the dough until they are evenly distributed and the beaten egg is absorbed.

SHAPING THE DOUGH

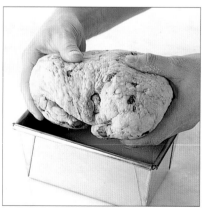

Follow the instructions on page 53 to gently shape the dough to fit the loaf tin. Place the dough into the buttered tin seam-side down.

PAIN TUNISIEN
TUNISIAN SEMOLINA AND OLIVE OIL BREAD

This golden, seeded bread is made with fine semolina, ground from North African durum wheat, which is also used to make couscous, the staple grain of the region. The soft, absorbent crumb is especially suited to soaking up the rich, spicy sauces of tagines, the full-flavoured, slow-simmered stews of northern Africa. This bread is perhaps best enjoyed as the heart of a simple meal, served with a bowl of olives, a few dates, and a plate of cubed white cheese.

USING A BREAD MACHINE
Use the dough setting (see pages 66–67). Remove the dough after rising and follow steps 5–8.

INGREDIENTS

2 tsp dried yeast

175ml (6fl oz) water

250g (8oz) semolina

250g (8oz) strong white flour

1½ tsp salt

125ml (4fl oz) olive oil

egg glaze, made with 1 egg yolk and 1 tbsp water (see page 58)

4 tbsp sesame seeds

1 Sprinkle the yeast into 100ml (3½fl oz) of the water in a bowl. Leave for 5 minutes; stir to dissolve. Mix the semolina, flour, and salt together in a large bowl. Make a well in the centre and pour in the yeasted liquid and the olive oil.

2 Mix in the flour. Stir in the remaining water, as needed, to form a stiff, sticky dough.

3 Turn out on to a floured work surface. Knead the dough until smooth and elastic, about 10 minutes.

4 Put the dough in a clean, oiled bowl and cover with a tea towel. Leave to rise until doubled in size, about 1–1½ hours.

5 Knock back, then leave to rest for 10 minutes. Divide the dough into two pieces. On a lightly floured work surface, shape each piece into a flattened round, 18cm (7in) across and 2.5cm (1in) thick.

6 Place the dough rounds on oiled baking sheets, then cover with a tea towel. Leave to prove until doubled in size, about 30–45 minutes.

7 Brush the tops of the dough rounds with the egg glaze and sprinkle evenly with sesame seeds. Prick all over with a skewer or toothpick to prevent air bubbles.

8 Bake in the preheated oven for 30 minutes until golden brown and hollow-sounding when tapped underneath. Cool on a wire rack.

 Rising
1–1½ hours
(see pages 50–51)

 Proving
30–45 minutes
(see page 57)

 Oven temperature
200°C/400°F/gas 6

 Baking
30 minutes
Steam optional
(see page 63)

 Yield
2 loaves

 Yeast alternative
15g (½oz)
fresh yeast
(see page 41)

BARBARI
PERSIAN SESAME BREAD

This light, crusty bread is Iran's favourite breakfast bread, especially when topped with crumbled white cheese and sprinkled with fresh herbs. When made with milk instead of water and sprinkled with sugar instead of sesame seeds, the bread is called Shirmal and is a much loved children's snack.

USING A BREAD MACHINE

Use the dough setting (see pages 66–67). Remove the dough after rising, brush it with oil, then follow steps 6–9.

INGREDIENTS

1 tsp runny honey

325ml (11fl oz) water

2 tsp dried yeast

500g (1lb) strong white flour

1½ tsp salt

2 tbsp olive oil, plus extra to glaze

2 tsp sesame seeds

1 Stir the honey into 175ml (6fl oz) of the water in a bowl, then sprinkle in the yeast. Leave for 5 minutes; stir to dissolve. Mix the flour and salt together in a large bowl. Make a well in the centre and pour in the yeasted mixture.

2 Use a wooden spoon to draw enough of the flour into the yeasted mixture to form a soft paste. Cover the bowl with a tea towel, then leave to "sponge" until frothy and risen, about 20 minutes.

3 Pour the remaining water, holding back about half, and the olive oil into the well. Mix in the rest of the flour. Stir in the reserved water, as needed, to form a firm, moist dough.

4 Turn the dough out on to a lightly floured work surface. Knead until smooth, shiny, and elastic, about 10 minutes.

5 Put the dough in a clean, oiled bowl, turning it to coat evenly with the oil, then cover with a tea towel. Leave to rise until doubled in size, about 1½–2 hours.

6 Knock back, then leave to rest for 10 minutes. Divide into four equal pieces. Shape each piece into a round 12cm (5in) across and 2.5cm (1in) thick. Cover with a tea towel and leave to prove until doubled in size, about 45 minutes.

7 Dust two baking sheets with flour and preheat in the oven until very hot, about 15 minutes.

8 Use your fingertips to gently press into the surface of the dough to form nine dimples, about 2cm (¾in) deep, across the top of each round. Brush each round with olive oil and sprinkle with sesame seeds.

9 Place the shaped dough on the hot baking sheets and bake in the preheated oven for 20 minutes until golden brown and hollow-sounding when tapped underneath. Leave to cool on a wire rack.

VARIATION
Spicy Seeded Persian Bread

• Make one quantity Barbari dough up to step 8, mixing 1 teaspoon paprika and ¼ teaspoon cayenne pepper into the flour in step 1.
• In step 8, dimple each round as instructed in the recipe.
• Brush the rounds with olive oil, then sprinkle 2 teaspoons each sesame seeds, poppy seeds, and cumin seeds evenly over the top of the four rounds.
• Preheat the oven to 220°C/425°F/gas 7. Place the shaped dough on the hot baking sheets and bake in the preheated oven for 20 minutes until golden and hollow-sounding when tapped underneath. Cool on a wire rack.

 To begin
Sponge method
Time: 20 minutes
(see page 44)

 Rising
1½–2 hours
(see pages 50–51)

 Proving
45 minutes
(see page 57)

 Oven temperature
220°C/425°F/gas 7

 Baking
20 minutes

 Yield
4 breads

 Yeast alternative
15g (½oz)
fresh yeast
(see page 41)

PIDE
TURKISH SEEDED BREAD POUCH

Pide *is baked in great quantities during the holy month of Ramadan. According to the Koran, bread was sent down to earth by God's command, and this soft, seeded bread is traditionally eaten at sundown to break the daily fast. Plain* Pide *is an accompaniment to grilled kebabs and* Köfte.

USING A BREAD MACHINE
Use the dough setting (see pages 66–67). Remove the dough after rising, brush it with oil, then follow steps 6–9.

INGREDIENTS

2 tsp dried yeast

½ tsp granulated sugar

325ml (11fl oz) water

500g (1lb) strong white flour

1 tsp salt

2 tbsp olive oil

egg glaze, made with 1 egg and 1 tbsp water (see page 58)

2 tsp nigella seeds

1 Sprinkle the yeast and sugar into 125ml (4fl oz) of the water in a bowl. Leave for 5 minutes, then stir to dissolve.

2 Sift the flour and salt together in a large bowl. Make a well in the centre and pour in the yeasted water and the olive oil.

3 Mix in the flour. Stir in the remaining water, as needed, to form a firm but soft dough.

4 Turn the dough out on to a lightly floured work surface. Knead until smooth, supple, and elastic, about 15 minutes. Initially, the dough will be quite stiff. It will soften and stretch gradually as you continue kneading.

5 Put the dough in a clean, oiled bowl, turning it to coat evenly with the oil. Cover with a tea towel, then leave to rise until doubled in size, about 1½ hours.

6 Knock back, then leave to rest for 10 minutes. Divide into two equal-sized pieces. Roll each piece into a smooth ball (*see page 55*). On a lightly floured work surface, roll out each piece of dough to form a round 25cm (10in) across, and 5mm (¼in) thick. Cover with a tea towel and leave to prove for 20 minutes.

7 Use the blunt edge of a knife to gently draw four parallel impressions across the top of each dough round, then four more impressions across the top in the opposite direction, to make a criss-cross pattern. Brush the rounds with the egg glaze.

8 Sprinkle the dough rounds evenly with nigella seeds, then place them on lightly floured baking sheets.

9 Bake in the preheated oven for 10–15 minutes until puffy and lightly coloured. Wrap the breads immediately in a tea towel to keep the crusts soft and to prevent drying out.

  Rising 1½ hours (*see pages 50–51*)

 Proving 20 minutes (*see page 57*)

 Oven temperature 220°C/425°F/gas 7

 Baking 10–15 minutes Steam optional (*see page 63*)

 Yield 2 breads

Yeast alternative 15g (½oz) fresh yeast (*see page 41*)

PIDE

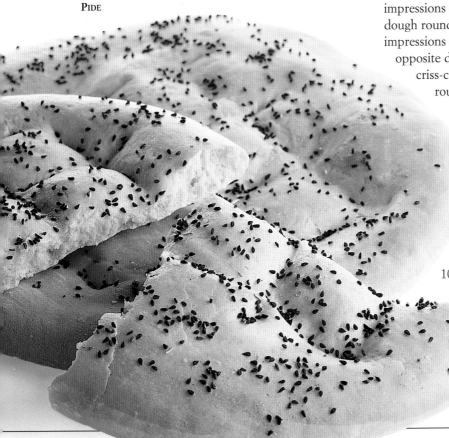

PAIN D'EPICE
FRENCH HONEY-SPICE BREAD

This aromatic bread dates from medieval times. It improves on keeping: for best results cool the bread in baking parchment, double wrap in foil, and store at room temperature for up to three days before eating.

USING A BREAD MACHINE
This recipe is not suitable for bread machines.

INGREDIENTS

1 tbsp oil, to grease tin

350ml (12fl oz) runny honey

40g (1½oz) dark brown sugar

125g (4oz) wholemeal flour

125g (4oz) rye flour

2 tsp baking powder

½ tsp ground cinnamon

½ tsp ground anise seeds

¼ tsp each ground star anise, grated nutmeg, ground cloves, ground ginger

zest of 1 orange, grated

2 eggs, beaten

100ml (3½fl oz) milk

1 Grease a 1kg (2lb) loaf tin with oil and line the sides and bottom of the tin with baking parchment. Put the honey and the sugar in a pan over a low heat and stir until viscous, about 3 minutes.

2 Sift the flours, baking powder, spices, and orange zest together in a large bowl. Make a well in the centre and pour in the eggs and milk.

3 Stir in the honey mixture, drawing in the flour to form a smooth batter. Pour the batter into the tin; it will be three-quarters full.

4 Bake in the preheated oven for 1¼ hours until dark and fragrant. Owing to its high sugar content, the loaf may need to be covered with foil to prevent burning, since the top will become very dark during cooking. The bread is ready when a metal skewer inserted into the centre comes out clean. Turn out of the loaf tin, and leave to cool on a wire rack.

  Oven temperature
220°C/425°F/gas 7

 Baking
1¼ hours

Yield
1 loaf

OLD ENGLISH CHEESE & APPLE LOAF

This moist and flavourful loaf, with its superlatively crunchy, cheesy crust, is perfect picnic and tea-time fare. Any apples you have on hand will do for this recipe, however crisp, sharp cooking apples like Granny Smith or Bramley are preferred.

USING A BREAD MACHINE
This recipe is not suitable for bread machines.

INGREDIENTS

1 tbsp oil, to grease tin

500g (1lb) plain flour

1 tbsp baking powder

½ tsp salt

60g (2oz) unsalted butter

4 apples, peeled, cored, and grated

125g (4oz) Cheddar, grated

2 eggs, beaten

rolled porridge oats, to sprinkle

1 Grease a 1kg (2lb) loaf tin with oil. Sift the flour, baking powder, and salt together in a large bowl.

2 Rub the butter into the flour mixture swiftly with your fingertips until the flour mixture resembles the texture of coarse breadcrumbs throughout.

3 Stir the grated apple and cheese into the flour and butter mixture. Add the beaten eggs and mix everything together until thoroughly blended.

4 Spoon the batter into the prepared tin and sprinkle the top with oats. Bake in the preheated oven for 1½–2 hours until golden brown and well-risen. The bread is ready when a metal skewer inserted into the centre comes out clean. Turn out of the loaf tin and leave to cool on a wire rack.

 Oven temperature
180°C/350°F/gas 4

 Baking
1½–2 hours

 Yield
1 loaf

NUTTY YOGURT BREAD

A ny well-stocked larder will furnish the ingredients for this useful all-purpose emergency loaf. Quick and easy to make, this crusty loaf studded with crunchy nuts and seeds is a perfect accompaniment to a bowl of steaming soup. Delicious when served warm from the oven, it also toasts exceptionally well.

USING A BREAD MACHINE
This recipe is not suitable for bread machines.

INGREDIENTS

1 tbsp sunflower oil, plus extra to grease tin

375g (13oz) plain flour

125g (4oz) wholemeal flour

1 tsp salt

1 tsp cream of tartar

1 tsp baking soda

1 tsp baking powder

90g (3oz) mixed nuts, chopped

90g (3oz) sunflower seeds

1 tsp runny honey

200ml (7fl oz) plain yogurt

300ml (½ pint) milk

2 tbsp sunflower seeds, for sprinkling

1 Grease a 1kg (2lb) loaf tin with oil. Sift the flours, salt, cream of tartar, baking soda, and baking powder together in a large bowl. Stir in the nuts and sunflower seeds.

2 Mix the honey, yogurt, milk, and oil together. Stir into the dry ingredients and mix to form a soft dough.

3 Spoon the batter into the prepared tin and smooth to level the top. Sprinkle with sunflower seeds. Bake in the preheated oven for 1 hour until golden and risen. The bread is ready when its edges shrink from the sides of the tin.

VARIATIONS
Seeded Yogurt Bread
• Make one quantity Nutty Yogurt Bread batter as directed in steps 1–2, replacing the nuts and sunflower seeds with 3 tablespoons each sesame and poppy seeds.

• Continue as directed in step 3. Sprinkle the top of the loaf with 2 teaspoons each sesame and poppy seeds in place of the sunflower seeds.

Herbed Yogurt Bread
• Make one quantity Nutty Yogurt Bread batter as directed in steps 1–2, replacing the nuts and seeds with 2 teaspoons dried mixed herbs (preferably *herbes de Provence*).
• Continue as directed in step 3. Sprinkle the top of the loaf with 3 tablespoons grated Cheddar in place of the sunflower seeds.

Oaten Yogurt Bread
• Make one quantity Nutty Yogurt Bread batter as directed in steps 1–2, replacing the plain flour with the same amount of medium oatmeal and omitting the nuts and seeds.
• Continue as directed in step 3. Sprinkle the top of the loaf with 2 tablespoons rolled porridge oats in place of the sunflower seeds.

Oven temperature
180°C/350°F/gas 4

Baking
1 hour

Yield
1 loaf

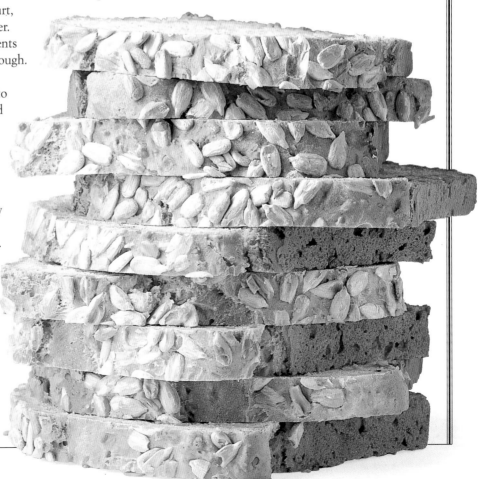

PAN DE MUERTO
"BREAD OF THE DEAD"

The staple flour in Mexico is cornmeal. Pan de Muerto, *which is baked specially for the Mexican Day of the Dead festival that takes place on All Souls' Day, is made instead with highly prized wheat flour. The bread is flavoured with orange water and anise seeds and decorated with pieces of dough formed into the shapes of bones. The bread is taken to the cemetery with other gifts including the symbolic flowers of the dead, yellow marigolds.*

USING A BREAD MACHINE

Use the dough setting (see pages 66–67). Remove the dough after rising and follow steps 6–8.

INGREDIENTS

2 tsp dried yeast

4 tbsp water

500g (1lb) plain flour

1 tsp salt

6 eggs, beaten

125g (4oz) unsalted butter, melted

125g (4oz) sugar

2 tsp anise seeds

1 tbsp orange flower water

zest of 1 orange, grated

egg glaze, made with 1 egg yolk beaten with 1 tbsp water (see page 58)

granulated sugar, to decorate

1 Sprinkle the yeast into the water in a bowl. Leave for 5 minutes; stir to dissolve. Mix the flour and salt together in a large bowl. Make a well in the centre of the flour and pour in the yeasted water.

2 Use a wooden spoon to draw enough of the flour into the yeasted water to form a soft paste. Cover with a tea towel and leave to "sponge" until frothy, about 20 minutes.

3 Add the eggs, butter, sugar, anise seeds, orange flower water, and orange zest to the flour well. Mix in the flour from the sides to form a soft, sticky dough.

4 Turn out on to a lightly floured work surface. Knead until smooth and elastic, 10 minutes.

5 Put the dough in a clean, buttered bowl, turning it to coat evenly with the butter. Leave to rise until doubled in size, about 2 hours.

6 Divide the dough into two equal pieces, and pinch off a quarter of each piece. Divide one of these small quarter pieces into two equal pieces and shape each one into a ball, 2.5cm (1in) across. Divide the other small quarter piece into 14 equal pieces, and shape each of these pieces into a cylinder, 1cm (½in) thick. Shape each cylinder into a small bone (*see below*).

7 Shape the two remaining large pieces of dough into two round loaves (*see page 54*). Place on a buttered baking sheet and stick one of the small balls on top of each loaf. Arrange the bones to form four crosses on the sides of each loaf.

8 Cover the shaped loaves with a tea towel and leave to prove until risen, about 30 minutes. Brush the loaves with the egg glaze and sprinkle with sugar. Bake in the preheated oven for 35 minutes until golden and hollow-sounding when tapped underneath. Cool on a wire rack. Sprinkle with granulated sugar.

To begin
Sponge method
Time: 20 minutes
(*see page 44*)

Rising
2 hours
(*see pages 50–51*)

Proving
30 minutes
(*see page 57*)

Oven temperature
180°C/350°F/gas 4

Baking
35 minutes

Yield
2 loaves

Yeast alternative
15g (½oz)
fresh yeast
(*see page 41*)

CIAMBELLA MANDORLATA
RING-SHAPED EASTER BREAD WITH NUT BRITTLE

Decorated with crunchy-sweet nut and spice topping, this Italian Easter bread is originally from Bologna, one of the capital cities of the Emilia Romagna region. This traditional ring-shaped loaf is said to represent the unity of the family. It is now common to see the bread in Italian bakeries all the year round, and not just during the Easter holidays.

USING A BREAD MACHINE

Use the dough setting (see pages 66–67). Remove the dough after rising and follow steps 5–8.

INGREDIENTS

2 tsp dried yeast

100ml (3½fl oz) tepid milk

600g (1¼lb) strong white flour

2 tsp salt

125g (4oz) granulated sugar

zest of 3 lemons, grated

125g (4oz) unsalted butter, softened

3 eggs, beaten

100ml (3½fl oz) water

for the topping

4 tsp ground cinnamon

3 tbsp granulated sugar

125g (4oz) blanched almonds, toasted and roughly chopped

1 egg yolk

1 Sprinkle the yeast into the milk in a small bowl. Leave for 5 minutes; stir to dissolve. Mix the flour, salt, sugar, and lemon zest together in a large bowl. Make a well in the centre of the mixture then add to it the butter, eggs, and the yeasted milk.

2 Mix in the flour from the sides of the well. Add the water, 1 tablespoon at a time as needed, to form a soft, sticky dough.

3 Turn the dough out on to a lightly floured work surface. Knead until smooth, springy, and elastic, about 10 minutes.

4 Put the dough in a clean bowl and cover. Leave to rise until doubled in size, about 4 hours.

5 Kock back the dough, then leave to rest, covered with a tea towel, for about 10 minutes.

6 Divide the dough into two equal pieces and roll each piece into a 40cm (16in) long rope. Twist the two dough ropes together.

7 Place the shaped dough rope on a buttered baking sheet. Shape it into a ring by bringing the two ends of the rope together. Pinch them to seal, and cover with a tea towel. Prove until doubled in size, about 1½ hours.

8 **To make the topping** Mix the cinnamon, sugar, almonds, and egg yolk together in a bowl. Use a rubber spatula to spread the mixture evenly over the top of the ring. Bake in the preheated oven for 45 minutes until golden and hollow-sounding when tapped underneath. Cool on a wire rack.

 Rising
4 hours
(*see pages 50–51*)

 Proving
1½ hours
(*see page 57*)

 Oven temperature
220°C/400°F/gas 6

 Baking
45 minutes

 Yield
1 loaf

 Yeast alternative
15g (½oz)
fresh yeast
(*see page 41*)

BOLO-REI
EPIPHANY BREAD

This bread is traditionally eaten in Portugal to celebrate the feast of the Epiphany – when the Three Kings arrived at Bethlehem.

USING A BREAD MACHINE

Use the dough setting (see pages 66–67). Remove the dough after rising and follow steps 6–8.

INGREDIENTS

100g (3½oz) glacé citrus peel, chopped

50g (1½oz) raisins

50g (1½oz) pine nuts

100ml (3½fl oz) port

2½ tsp dried yeast

100ml (3½fl oz) water

500g (1lb) strong white flour

1½ tsp salt

100g (3½oz) unsalted butter, softened

100g (3½oz) caster sugar

zest of 1 lemon and 1 orange

3 eggs, beaten

a dried broad bean and a small present

for the topping

egg glaze, made with 1 egg yolk beaten with 1 tbsp water (see page 58)

10 glacé cherries

2 segments each glacé orange, lemon, and lime peel

lump sugar, crushed, to decorate

apricot jam, to glaze

1 Soak the glacé peel, raisins, and pine nuts in the port overnight. Sprinkle the yeast into the water in a bowl. Leave for 5 minutes; stir to dissolve. Mix the flour and salt together in a large bowl. Make a well in the centre and pour in the yeasted water.

2 Use a wooden spoon to draw enough of the flour into the yeasted water to form a soft paste. Cover the bowl with a tea towel. Leave to "sponge" until frothy and slightly risen, about 20 minutes.

3 Beat the butter with the sugar and lemon and orange zest together in a separate bowl until light and fluffy. Add the eggs, one at a time, and beat well after each addition. Add the mixture to the flour well, then mix in the flour from the sides to form a soft dough.

4 Turn the dough out on to a lightly floured work surface. Knead until soft, smooth, silky, and elastic, about 10 minutes. Knead in the peel, raisins, and pine nuts until evenly distributed (*see page 99*).

5 Put the dough in a clean bowl and cover with a tea towel. Leave to rise until doubled in size, about 2 hours.

6 Knock back, then leave to rest for 10 minutes. Shape into a *couronne* (*see page 56*), then place it on a buttered baking sheet. Wrap a dried broad bean and a trinket or small present separately in grease-proof paper. Insert both packages in the bottom of the shaped dough.

7 Cover the dough with a tea towel, and leave to prove until doubled in thickness, about 1 hour.

8 **To make the topping** Brush the dough with the egg glaze then decorate with the glacé fruit and the crushed sugar. Bake in a preheated oven for 45 minutes until golden. Warm the apricot jam in a saucepan over low heat until liquid, then brush the top and sides of the bread with it to glaze. Leave to cool on a wire rack.

To begin
Sponge method
Time: 20 minutes
(*see page 44*)

Rising
2 hours
(*see pages 50–51*)

Proving
1 hour
(*see page 57*)

Oven temperature
180°C/350°F/gas 4

Baking
45 minutes

Yield
1 loaf

Yeast alternative
20g (¾oz) fresh yeast
(*see page 41*)

BREAD & BUTTER PUDDING

This old-fashioned favourite was originally made with leftover, plain white or brown bread, but *Victorian Milk Bread Brioche, Challah, or Panettone can be used for more indulgent versions. Try the chocolate variation for a wickedly delicious pudding. Make with any of the breads suggested or try it with Cinnamon Raisin Bread for a real treat. Soak the raisins in dark rum for a lusciously boozy twist – Chocolate, Rum, and Raisin Bread Pudding.*

INGREDIENTS

32 slices Baguette, or 8 slices tin loaf

30g (1oz) unsalted butter, softened

100g (3½oz) raisins

zest of 1 lemon, grated

¼ tsp ground nutmeg, plus extra to dust

3 eggs, beaten

3 tbsp caster sugar

500ml (17fl oz) milk

125ml (3½fl oz) double cream

1 tsp vanilla extract

icing sugar, to dust

1 Butter each slice of bread on one side. If using tin loaf slices, cut each one in half diagonally, then into quarters. Scatter 1 tablespoon of raisins over the bottom of a buttered, 1 litre (1¾ pint), oval baking dish.

2 Layer the buttered bread in the baking dish, sprinkling raisins, lemon zest, and nutmeg between each layer. Make sure that the top layer of bread is placed with the buttered side up.

3 Put the eggs and 2 tablespoons of the sugar in a large bowl. Heat the milk, cream, and vanilla extract in a saucepan over a medium heat, until just boiling. Whisk the hot milk and cream mixture into the eggs and sugar to make a custard; pour over the bread. Lightly press down the bread slices to completely submerge them in the custard.

4 Dust with nutmeg and 1 tablespoon of sugar. Cover the baking dish with a piece of greaseproof paper. Leave to soak for 20–30 minutes.

5 Bake in the preheated oven, covered, for 20 minutes. Remove the paper from the pudding and bake for a further 20–25 minutes until the custard has just set, the pudding has risen up slightly, and the bread slices have turned crispy around the edges. Dust with icing sugar and serve warm.

VARIATION
Chocolate Bread Pudding

• Make one quantity Bread & Butter Pudding up to step 2.

• Omit the lemon zest and replace the nutmeg with 1 teaspoon ground cinnamon. Arrange the bread in the dish as directed in step 2, sprinkling the raisins, cinnamon, and 100g (3½oz) plain chocolate, roughly chopped, between each layer.

• Put the eggs and sugar in a large bowl. Heat the milk, cream, and vanilla as directed in step 3; remove from the heat and add 100g (3½oz) chopped chocolate. Leave to stand for 5 minutes, then whisk until the chocolate has completely melted.

• Whisk the chocolate mixture into the eggs and sugar, then pour over the bread. Press the bread slices down into the mixture. Omitting the nutmeg, soak, bake, and serve, as directed in steps 4–5.

Oven temperature
220°C/425°F/gas 7

Baking
40–45 minutes

Makes
4–6 servings

BREADS TO USE

Pain Ordinaire, page 72

Victorian Milk Bread, page 76

Ballymaloe Brown Bread, page 78

Baguette, page 79

Brioche, page 112

Zopf, page 117

Pain Viennois, page 117

Challah, page 150

Pulla, page 150

Panettone, page 155

BREADCRUMBS & CROUTONS

BREADS TO USE FOR BREADCRUMBS

•

BREADS TO USE FOR CROUTES

•

BREADS TO USE FOR DICED CROUTONS

•

BREADS TO USE FOR MELBA TOAST

•

BREADS TO USE FOR SHAPED CROUTONS

SHAPED CROUTONS

LA CHAPELURE

DRIED BREADCRUMBS

The primary use of dried breadcrumbs is as a coating for ingredients to be deep-fried or roasted. Foods to be fried are usually dipped first in flour and then in beaten egg before being dipped in breadcrumbs. Ingredients such as fish fillets or rack of lamb are often spread with a little smooth mustard before the breadcrumbs are pressed on. Stored in an airtight container, dried breadcrumbs keep indefinitely.

Makes 125g (4oz) dried breadcrumbs

125g (4oz) slices day-old bread, crusts cut off

Put the bread slices on a baking sheet. Leave in a 150°C/ 300°F/gas 2 oven until dry and crisp, about 10 minutes. Let cool.
To grind by hand Wrap the bread in a plastic bag. Press a rolling pin all over the bag, crushing the bread until ground to the desired consistency. Press through a sieve for a finer texture.
To grind in a food processor or blender Put the dried bread in the work bowl of a food processor, or in a blender. Pulse to grind to the desired consistency.

VARIATION
Chapelure à la Provençale
• Make one quantity dried breadcrumbs.
• In a small bowl combine the dried breadcrumbs with 2 finely chopped garlic cloves, 3 tablespoons olive oil, 1 tablespoon fresh thyme leaves, a pinch each salt and pepper, and 4 tablespoons chopped parsley.
• Use to coat meat or fish before sprinkling with olive oil and roasting or grilling at a high temperature.

LA PANURE

FRESH BREADCRUMBS

Fresh breadcrumbs have two main roles. In stuffings, forcemeats, dumplings, and steamed puddings, breadcrumbs bind the ingredients together. When sprinkled as a topping over gratins and other baked dishes, breadcrumbs provide both colour and crunch and serve to protect creamy sauces from the high heat of the oven or grill. Fresh breadcrumbs can be stored in an air-tight container and frozen for up to six months.

Makes 150g (5oz) fresh breadcrumbs

150g (5oz) slices fresh bread, crusts cut off

To chop by hand Use a chef's knife to cut the bread into cubes on a large chopping board. Chop the bread cubes coarsely or finely as stipulated in the recipe.
To grind in a food processor or blender Cut the bread into rough chunks; put in the work bowl of a food processor, or a blender. Pulse the machine to grind the bread to the desired consistency.

VARIATIONS
Panure à la Milanaise
• Make one quantity fresh breadcrumbs.
• Mix with 60g (2oz) grated Parmesan.
• Use to top gratin dishes before baking or grilling at a high temperature.

Buttered Crumbs
• Make one quantity fresh breadcrumbs.
• Melt 60g (2oz) butter in a pan over a medium heat. When the butter is hot, add the breadcrumbs and stir well to coat evenly. Sauté until golden, about 1 minute.
• Use to top steamed vegetables.

CROUTES

Croûtes *make ideal canapé bases for savoury toppings like fresh goat's cheese. They are also an essential component of the classic, Parisian, bistro-style recipe* Soupe à L'Ognion Gratinée. Crostini *are simply the Italian (originally Tuscan) equivalent of the French* Croûtes.

Makes about 32 croûtes

1 day-old Baguette

Preheat the oven to 180°C/ 350°F/gas 4. Cut the Baguette into 1cm (½in) slices. Place slices in a single layer on a baking sheet. Bake until crisp, about 15 minutes. Use for canapé bases or with antipasti.

VARIATIONS
Cheese Croûtes
• Make one quantity Croûtes as directed.
• Melt 30g (1oz) butter. Grate 30g (1oz) Parmesan. Brush one side of each croûte with the butter or alternatively with oil.
• Sprinkle the grated cheese and a pinch of cayenne pepper evenly over the buttered side of each croûte. Place in a single layer on a baking sheet and bake for 5 minutes more, until golden.
• Use as a garnish for soups or salads.

Garlic Croûtes
• Make one quantity Croûtes as directed.
• Peel 1 garlic clove and cut it in half.
• Rub one side of each croûte with the cut side of the garlic. Sprinkle this side of each of the croûtes with olive oil.
• Use as a garnish for soups or salads.

DICED CROUTONS

Diced Croûtons *add a delicious crunch to soups, salads, and omelettes. They are best when made just before serving, but may be prepared several hours ahead and kept at room temperature. To reheat, place in an oven, 160°C/325°F/gas 3, for 5 minutes.*

Makes about 40 croûtons

4 slices day-old bread, crusts cut off

30g unsalted butter and 2 tbsp sunflower oil

To fry Cut the bread into 1cm (½in) cubes. Heat the butter and oil in a frying pan over a low heat. Test that it is hot enough by adding one cube to the pan; the bread should sizzle when it goes in. Place the cubes in the pan in a single layer. Sauté, stirring constantly, for about 10 minutes until crisp. Drain on kitchen towels before serving. Leave to cool.

Makes about 40 croûtons

4 slices day-old bread, crusts cut off

30g unsalted butter, melted

To bake Preheat the oven to 200°C/400°F/gas 6. Cut the bread into 1cm (½in) cubes; place in a roasting dish. Pour the melted butter over the cubes and toss them to coat evenly. Bake until crisp and golden, about 10 minutes.

VARIATION
Garlic Croûtons
• Make one quantity Diced Croûtons by either method as directed; remove from the frying pan or oven just before they are done.
• Toss with 1 finely chopped garlic clove while still hot and before draining.
• Return to a hot frying pan or oven for a couple of minutes to finish crispening.

MELBA TOAST

These *wafer-thin slices of toast make a perfect accompaniment to pâtés, potted meats, creamy dips and, best of all, caviar. They can be stored in an airtight container for several days; reheat before serving.*

Makes about 32 toasts

4 slices bread, each about 1cm (½in) thick

Preheat the oven to 180°C/ 350°F/gas 4. Toast the bread slices. Cut off the crusts and slice each piece of toast in half horizontally to make two slices from one. Cut each slice in half diagonally and in half again to make small triangle shapes. Place on a baking sheet and bake for 10 minutes until golden, crisp, and curled.

SHAPED CROUTONS

These *elegant, parsley-tipped shapes are used in French* haute cuisine *as a classic garnish.*

Makes about 12 heart-shaped croûtons

4 slices bread, each about ½cm (¼in) thick

30g (1oz) unsalted butter

2 tbsp sunflower oil

1 tbsp finely chopped parsley, optional

Cut the bread into heart-shaped pieces. Heat the butter and oil in a frying pan over a low heat. Add the bread shapes to the pan in a single layer. Sauté for about 5 minutes on each side until golden. If desired, dip the pointed ends of the croutons in the finely chopped parsley.

PROBLEM SOLVING

A LESS THAN PERFECT LOAF of bread generally begins with a less than perfect dough. In fact, the most common mistake in breadmaking is producing a dough that is too dry. A dry dough is stiff and hard and will remain a solid, heavy lump that will resist proper kneading, rising, proving, and shaping. It is impossible to specify an exact quantity of liquid, or indeed precise rising times, for each recipe when flour, temperature, and humidity vary so greatly from kitchen to kitchen, and region to region. Carefully follow the recipe instructions for dough consistency, as well as the kneading, rising, and proving times. However, remember that bread dough is influenced by its environment. Therefore, it is important to take this factor into account and adjust the instructions as necessary. Use these guidelines to help make a perfect dough.

ACHIEVING THE RIGHT CONSISTENCY

THE IDEAL CONSISTENCY for most doughs is firm but moist. A dough should feel soft and slightly sticky after mixing, but should become smooth and elastic as it is kneaded. Resist adding extra flour until you are certain that the dough is unmanageable. Adjustments are best made at the mixing stage, but additional water or flour can be added to the dough at the kneading stage as well.

DRY DOUGH AT THE MIXING STAGE

1 The bulk of the flour and the water gathers together into a ball but also leaves a crumbly mass at the bottom of the mixing bowl. Add water, 1 teaspoon at a time, to the dry crumbs.

2 Use a wooden spoon to mix the dry crumbs with the water until a smooth paste is formed. Combine this mixture with the main bulk of the dough by kneading the two together with your hands.

DRY DOUGH AT THE KNEADING STAGE

THE DOUGH HAS BEEN gathered to form a ball but is still too stiff and hard to knead. Add water gradually to allow the dough to absorb the liquid without becoming a slippery, sticky mess. A water sprayer with a fine mist is best for this purpose. Spray the dough and continue kneading; repeat until you achieve the required consistency. If you do not have a water sprayer, moisten your hands lightly with water and knead. Repeat, if necessary.

WET DOUGH AT THE KNEADING STAGE

THE DOUGH IS REQUIRED to be firm enough to hold its shape after kneading. In most recipes it should become more pliable as it is kneaded: your fingers should come away as you knead and it should feel smooth and light. However, if the dough is still too wet to work with, extra flour can be added at the kneading stage. Dust the dough lightly with flour and continue kneading; dust again with more flour, only if necessary.

COMMON PROBLEMS IN BAKED BREADS

PROBLEM	POSSIBLE CAUSES	REMEDIES
CLOSE-TEXTURED, DENSE CRUMB	• The dough was too dry. It should feel soft and sticky after mixing. If dry, it will not develop.	• *Follow the instructions to achieve the required dough consistency given in the recipe. See instructions on the opposite page for adding additional liquid at either the mixing or the kneading stage.*
	• The dough was not sufficiently kneaded. It should feel smooth and elastic after kneading.	• *To test the dough for sufficient kneading, press it with a fingertip. The indent made with your finger should spring back immediately. If it does not, continue to knead until it is ready.*
	• The dough had not risen sufficiently. It should rise until it is doubled in size, puffy, and aerated.	• *Check the dough after rising to be sure that it has risen properly. Use the test illustrated below to determine if more time is necessary.* • *To ensure that rising is complete, test the dough by gently pressing it with a fingertip (see right). If the dough has risen properly it will not spring back completely. The dough will spring back at once if the rising is not complete.*
A FLAT AND SPREAD-OUT LOAF	• The dough was over-proved, causing the loaf to collapse from the initial exposure to the heat of the oven during baking. When dough is very puffed up and more than doubled in size (unless specified in the recipe) it is over-proved.	• *Knock the shaped dough back, reshape it, and leave to prove again. If the recipe requires the dough to be so soft that it does not hold its shape, use a basket to support the loaf while proving.* • *To test for over-proving press the dough with a fingertip. If the dough has been over-proved it will deflate and release a strong smell of fermenting yeast.*
CRACKS ON SIDES OF LOAF	• The dough was under-proved, causing the loaf to expand too much in the oven. The loaf burst open during baking after the outer crust had already formed.	• *Leave the shaped dough to prove until it has doubled in volume and is light, puffy, and aerated. Test the dough for sufficient proving by gently pressing it with a fingertip – if the dough does not form an indentation or springs back quickly it requires more proving time. If an indentation is made and then springs back gradually but completely, the dough is ready to be placed in the oven.*
	• The dough was improperly shaped or the seam was not sealed well at the end of shaping.	• *Review basic shaping (see pages 52–57). Be sure to always apply pressure evenly at the various steps of shaping a loaf and to allow the dough to rest in between steps should it begin to resist or tighten.*
DRY PATCHES OF UNCOOKED DOUGH	• The dough was left either uncovered or in a draughty place during the rising or the proving steps of the recipe.	• *Cover the dough securely with a tea towel (see right) and avoid draughty places while rising and proving. Discard any dry, crusty pieces that have formed on top of the dough before shaping.*

GLOSSARY

Anise seeds green-brown, oval seeds with an aromatic liquorice flavour. Native to the Middle East, anise seeds are widely available in most supermarkets.

Batter a mixture of flour, liquid, and sometimes leaven that can be thick or thin, but is of spooning or pouring consistency.

Biga Italian for a starter. Traditionally fermented for a minimum of 12 hours, it produces a bread with a lightly fermented taste, and an open, porous texture.

Boule French for ball, referring to a round loaf of white bread also called *miche*.

Bread dough a mixture of flour, liquid, and often leaven, used to make bread. The required consistency of bread dough varies according to the recipe instructions and the desired texture and appearance of the loaf, but it should generally be stiff enough to work easily with the hands.

Brioche traditional French bread dough enriched with butter and eggs. The classic shape, called *Brioche à Tête*, is round and has a fluted base and a top knot.

Brot the German word for bread.

Buttermilk an ingredient made by adding special bacteria to skimmed or semi-skimmed milk, giving it a slightly thickened texture and tangy flavour. If unavailable, it can be substituted with the following mixture: 1 tablespoon lemon juice or cider vinegar, plus enough semi-skimmed milk to make up 250ml (8oz). Stir, then let stand for 5 minutes. This will yield 250ml (8fl oz).

Chafe to shape a risen dough into a round by using your hands to apply a downwards pressure to the sides of the dough while at the same time rotating it at the base.

Crust the hardened outer layer of, most commonly, a cooked food such as bread.

Dough a stiff but pliable mixture of flour, liquid, and other ingredients. This mixture remains a dough until it has been baked.

Fermentation a process during which carbohydrates go through a chemical change caused by enzymes produced from bacteria, micro-organisms, or yeast.

Ghee a term for concentrated, clarified butter with a strong, sweet flavour, used as a cooking fat in India and many Arab countries.

Gluten the stretchy elastic strands of protein that form when wheat flour is mixed with water and kneaded. It causes a bread dough to rise by trapping the carbon dioxide given off by the yeast and creates a network of bubbles in the crumb of the baked loaf.

Grease to prepare a bread tin or mould by brushing the inside with oil or butter before adding a dough or batter. This prevents the bread from sticking during baking.

Herbes de Provence an aromatic blend of dried herbs that grow in the Provence region of France; these usually include thyme, rosemary, bay, basil, savory, marjoram, lavender, and fennel seeds. It is available in speciality stores and some supermarkets.

Jalapeño a dark green variety of chilli that may vary from medium hot to very hot in flavour. Measures about 5cm (2in) long and 2cm (1in) wide, and has a rounded tip.

Key a term used to describe the final seam produced in a piece of dough once it has been folded and shaped into a loaf.

Kirsch a clear fruit brandy distilled from whole cherries. Used both as a digestive liqueur and as a flavouring in baking.

Knead to work a dough by rhythmically pushing, stretching, and folding it in order to develop the gluten in the flour.

Knock back to deflate a fully risen dough by pressing down on it and literally forcing the air out before the dough is shaped.

Leaven an agent such as yeast or baking powder that is added to baked goods to lighten the texture and increase the volume.

Leavened a word describing baked goods that contain a rising agent.

Linseeds also known as flax seeds, these tiny, oval, shiny brown seeds are rich in nutrients and are available from health-food stores.

Nigella seeds available in Middle Eastern, Indian, and other speciality stores, these tiny black seeds with a nutty flavour are sometimes called black onion seeds.

Orange-flower water distilled from fresh orange blossoms, this perfumed flavouring is available in Middle Eastern, Indian, and other speciality stores.

Pain the French word for bread.

Pane the Italian word for bread.

Paste a mixture of flour, liquid, and sometimes a leaven, which is too stiff to pour but too moist to work with the hands.

Poolish French for a starter. Traditionally fermented for a minimum of 2 hours, it produces a bread with a light, springy texture and a nutty aroma.

Prosciutto also sold under the name Parma Ham, this unsmoked, Italian ham has been pressed, salt-cured, and air-dried.

Proving also referred to as the final rise, this is the process during which a shaped dough is left to rise just before baking.

Rising the process during which a dough is aerated by carbon dioxide gas produced by a leavening agent before and during baking, causing it to grow in volume.

Sift to pass dry ingredients through a fine sieve in order to incorporate air and to make them lighter and more even in texture.

Slash to make incisions in the surface of a risen dough before baking to allow the loaf to rise and expand as it bakes without tearing or cracking the outer crust.

Sourdough, Sourdough bread a bread with a slightly sour, tangy flavour created by using a sourdough starter as the leaven.

Sourdough starter (see Starter) a starter that has been left to ferment for at least 48 hours. It produces a bread with a unique, slightly sour, tangy flavour.

Sponging the process by which a period of fermentation is added during the mixing stage, to produce a bread with a light crumb and a faintly yeasty aroma.

Star Anise available in Asian and speciality stores, this star-shaped spice has a strong, sweet aniseed flavour. It is a key ingredient in Chinese five-spice powder.

Starter a mixture of flour, yeast, and water, left to ferment for 2 hours to 5 days, and up to 2 weeks. It is used as an alternative rising agent to yeast, on its own, to leaven a bread dough. It is added to the flour at the mixing step when making a bread dough and affects both the taste and texture of bread.

Unleavened a word describing baked foods that contain no rising agent.

INDEX

USEFUL ADDRESSES

Speciality Flour Suppliers
Marriage's Flour,
Chelmsford Chelmer Mills
and Brick Barns Farm Ltd.,
Chelmsford,
Essex CM1 1PN
Tel: 01245 354455
Mail order service.

Shipton Mill,
Long Newnton,
Tetbury,
Gloucester GL8 8RP
Tel: 01665 505050
Mail order service.

Dove's Farm,
Salisbury Road,
Hungerford,
Berkshire RG17 0RF
Tel: 01488 684880
Mail order service.

Little Salkeld Watermill,
Penrith,
Cumbria CA10 1NN
Tel: 01768 881523
Mail order service.

**Information on Flour and
Breadmaking**
Flour Advisory Bureau Ltd.,
21 Arlington Street,
London SW1A 1RN
Tel: 0171 493 2521

**Speciality Breadmaking
Equipment**
Divertimenti,
139 Fulham Road,
London SW3
Tel: 0171 386 9911
Mail order service.

Alan Silverwood Ltd.,
Ledsam Street,
Ledsam House,
Birmingham B16 8DN

French Baguette Trays
David Mellor,
4 Sloane Square,
London SW1 8EE
Tel: 0171 730 4259
Mail order service.

**Spices and Speciality
Ingredients**
The Spice Shop,
1 Blenheim Crescent,
London W11 2EE
Tel: 0171 221 4448
Mail order service.

**Breadmaking Classes for
Adults and Children**
Books For Cooks,
4 Blenheim Crescent,
London W11 1NN
Tel: 0171 221 1992

ACKNOWLEDGMENTS

AUTHORS' ACKNOWLEDGMENTS
It may only take a little time to make an honest loaf, but this book would not have been possible without the help, patience, understanding, passion, and support of a number of people.

Eric Treuille would like to thank Julia Pemberton Hellums for keeping everything together and for invaluable information about American breads and flours, Julia Brock for helping with German breads, and Didier Lascaze, my wonderful traditional baker and friend in Cahors, for helping me immeasurably to understand real breadmaking. Heidi Lascelles who is always there for us with support, love, and enthusiasm for all enterprises at Books For Cooks, whether it be late-night recipe testing and tasting, baking workshops, or teaching nursery school children the basics of breadmaking. Peter and Juliet Kindersley for the use of their kitchen, weekend after weekend, for bringing us back breads from their travels all over the world, and for allowing the collaboration of the "ladies" in the arduous task of quality control. The DK and studio teams for their creativity, energy, and good will in this especially challenging project. Ursula for never letting us down with her enthusiasm and driving passion for this book and everything to do with breadmaking. Finally, special thanks to my wife Rose, because she made this book not just possible, but the ultimate of its kind.

Ursula Ferrigno would like to thank Julia Pemberton Hellums for her outstanding editing and dedication to our book. I am thrilled for her total involvement every step of the way, and for her encouragement and persistence for a great result. Rosie Kindersley, not only for her excellent eye but also for her determination for this book to be better than any other; her researching and energy are boundless. Ian O'Leary: it has been so delightful working with him in his fabulous studio and with Emma, his assistant – his photographs are amazing. Hilary Krag and Gurinder Purewall, for their great design work. My family, as always, for their power of listening and advice and help with research. My man in Rome for just being him, and his help with my dreadful spelling. Kate O'Donnel for recipe testing so diligently in the heat of the summer. Books For Cooks for allowing me to be there for all the fun and support, particularly Heidi Lascelles the owner. My co-author for his determination and amazing food-styling eye.

PUBLISHER'S ACKNOWLEDGMENTS
Dorling Kindersley would like to thank Neff U.K. Ltd. for the use of one of their ovens, Kitchen Aid for the donation of their appliances, Shipton Mills for their generous donations of flour and plant specimens, The Flour Advisory Board for help with flour research, Nicola Nieburg for editorial assistance, Susan Bosanko for the index, Christine Rista for picture research, and make-up artist Sue Sian.

Picture Credits
Key to pictures: t = top, c = centre, b = bottom, l = left, r = right.

The publisher would like to thank the following for their kind permission to reproduce the following photographs: Musée de la Ville de Paris, Musée Carnavalet, Paris 12tl; Mary Evans Picture Library 16tl; AKG London 18tl; Dover Publications 22tl; Ann Ronan Picture Library 24tl.

Photography by Ian O'Leary, except: David Murray and Jules Selmes 27c; Martin Cameron 34tr; Clive Streeter 96cl, 101r; Steve Gorton 99cl; Dave King 115cr; Philip Dowell 144br.